Narcissism & Psychopathy

A Book About Those Who Never Find True Happiness – and Their Children

Eva Traff

Table of Contents

Acknowledgements

My wonderful family – you're my sail and my lifeline. Thank you for all your patience and all the love you have given me while I was sitting in front of the computer working with this book.

I want to give a heartfelt thanks to all those who have read and reflected on the contents of this book. No one performs the best in solitude! Your support and strength are very important to me. Also, publishing this book wouldn't have been possible without the cooperation and support of my colleagues at Savvybookmarketing.

I would also like to extend my thanks to those of you who contributed your knowledge and experience of a life spent with dark secrets. You are extremely important in the struggle against the mental illness that is spreading in the wake of narcissism and psychopathy. Promise me, and the readers of this book, never to be silent! You are among the people who have understood the following quote by *Sandy Hotchkiss*:

"Our culture is full of narcissistic influences that numb us to the reality of the problems we face. To fight back, we need strong, real selves that are capable of transcending mere self-interest. When we understand where self-esteem really comes from and make a commitment to raising

healthy children – when this becomes our number one priority - we will have turned the corner towards a better world."

Preface

Writing this book has been difficult. I have had to live in the past to write about my father and his lifelong suffering. My father was a man stuck in a narcissistic personality who ultimately took his own life. My biggest wish is that my father's struggle was not in vain, that his experiences contribute to change. This struggle is about so much more than my family and me.

In my father's last handwritten note, he referred to his life as a bad chapter. Despite this, he invested in himself all his life at the expense of the rest of us. He lived in constant fear of not being good enough. He needed to be a man on top of the world. He showed it through his narcissistic defence, which also went out over the rest of us. He wasted many precious years, as did we. I don't want to use the term personality disorder alone. I also want to say personality destroyed. His own life was overshadowed by his father's abuse since his birth.

Just as we once were, many people are in urgent need of the support and information that this book is intended to provide. These include the children of narcissistic and/or psychopathic parents and those with other disorders, diagnoses, and addictions that affect mental wellbeing.

These children will grow up to be our children's present and future fellow human beings. Sixty-nine people, mostly young, were murdered on Utøya Island in Norway on July 22nd, 2011. Anders Behring Breivik, the terrorist, should have grown up to be one of them. Instead, he grew up to be a monster. He was the last one they ever saw. Breivik is one of the examples mentioned in this book.

Personality disorders germinate in childhood, and there is a great risk that it spreads further and further as a direct result of human ignorance. I hope this book will reach those living in terrible situations without understanding their problem. They do not know that they are living close to a person with a personality disorder.

When mum and I lowered dad's urn, I asked for forgiveness from him for writing this book. But if one brave person close to him as a child had read a book like this one, he might be alive today. He might even have been a loving and present father and grandfather.

Introduction

"Do not bother unless you are serious."
"One bad chapter does not mean the end of your story."

These words are, as far as I know, my Dad's last written words. On a beautiful summer day in July 2018, he chose to end his life.

The words were written on a note left on his kitchen table. I interpret these words as if it was a wish he had. Perhaps, he was hoping for rebirth. He wanted a new chance in another life.

After his death, I have been told that he regretted certain things he did in life, but he never told his family about it. He did not give himself or us a chance for reconciliation before he left earthly life. However, I have been reconciled with Dad after writing this book. I have received explanations for everyone's fate. Unfortunately, such a reconciliation wouldn't be possible if he were to live again but still be unchanged. For the man he had been, I would not have wanted him in my life that way. But at least, now, I have reconciled with him in thought and in sorrow. As far as I know, there still is no research showing transmigration as a fact. Probably, this was the only life he got the chance to and the only life he lived.

Whether we believe in rebirth or not, I may be able to give his life meaning afterwards. I do not want his story, nor mine, to be in vain. Everything that has happened in my family cannot be without meaning because if it is, it becomes a wound that can never heal.

I have been studying psychology at the university as well as in counselling with professionals. From that, I have understood that my dad was a person with a narcissistic personality disorder. It is important to be very careful in using these terms, but there is no doubt. The problem is that a narcissistic person very seldom would accept professional help to receive a diagnosis. Though, when you have experienced many years with a person suffering from a personality disorder, it's quite visible to you. You understand such a personality even more when you get a chance to get away from your life for a while, experience a different world after a long time and from that, receive new impressions and more knowledge.

Living with a person suffering from a personality disorder often leads to many family secrets, sometimes undiscovered ones, even to the family members themselves.

Children who only have their family experiences to grow into and who have not experienced anything else do not know things should not be this way. How would they know? They have not seen anything different in their entire lives. Perhaps, the saddest thing of all is that a person with a disorder of this kind can lead their family members to believe that the problem lies within themselves. Everything is their fault. They are "wrong." So secrets cannot surface nor be questioned. Instead, everything ends with no one in the family having any self-esteem. No one in the family is well, but no one in the family knows why.

I made the decision an early fall morning, when I was nineteen, after a big quarrel with my dad, to pack my most important possessions and leave my home. I never moved back.

I ended my social heritage (a pattern of career, choices, habits and behaviours inherited from my family and relatives), and I think my rescue was that I loved school. My dream was to become a teacher. I had chosen my career many years earlier. I was determined. Despite my anxiety, my eating disorders, my low self-esteem, social insecurity, and stress disorders, my path would be straight. *I would become a teacher.* During my studies, I got to see another world. I got to learn things that opened my eyes.

When I had my children, I made a second big break by writing my book *Safe Harbour – Building Self-esteem with Parenting, Love and Understanding.* Since then, I have understood what really happened during this time of my life. I stopped my social heritage big time! My children wouldn't suffer any negative impact through me as a result of this legacy. My children would grow up in a better environment than the one I grew up in, or the one that my dad suffered through or the one my grandfather survived.

For such behaviours or ways of life, there are always explanations that arise out of past experiences. I know it wasn't easy for my grandfather to grow up either. To be a child in a rough world is never a good thing. It is difficult to point out who is the victim and who is the perpetrator when it comes to a legacy that continues from one generation to the next.

So, what is the explanation for my dad's personality? I needed to know that as part of my therapy. I needed explanations, still do. More than I've already got. I remember this one night in my early teens. It was the single time he had ever said anything to me in person about his own childhood and his parents, my grandparents. My grandfather had a crick, and my dad, therefore, carved a cane for him. It hurts a lot to think about this young, empathic boy who grew up only to be destroyed. My dad had to witness his father when he abused his mother, my dear grandmother, with that very same cane. Dad was drunk when he told me this. The single time I ever saw tears in his eyes was this night. I remember very clearly when he leaned towards me and said, *"And I made that cane."* I also know that my grandmother sometimes hid in the woods at night to protect herself from my grandfather. She once told me that she was beaten during one of her pregnancies.

Grandmother being abused with the cane is one of the many experiences my dad lived through as a child, experiences that *explain*. If I had known better at the time, I would have asked more, made him talk and talk and talk. Maybe then he would have let his tears out, but as a teenager, I sat petrified and had no idea what to say. Dad had his sorrows in life, major ones, but he never got any help in dealing with them. The grief poisoned him, psychologically and emotionally. This poisoning, unfortunately, spread, both within himself and to the rest of us.

I have chosen a totally different way to handle problems in life. Ever since I was a young adult, I have never been quiet if I experienced difficulties. Even though I did not know why I suffered from eating disorders in my late teens, I finally sought help. To not stay quiet when there is something that feels wrong is very good advice. I talked to curators and some friends. I detoxified myself. There is always someone who can listen to you. Always.

This book is about a very grand and very difficult topic. I still want to make my contribution to raising awareness by sharing my experiences, the experiences of others and the research I have been studying. People's experiences should not be in vain. Researchers' efforts and the knowledge they create must spread. Their results should be used to help everyone who is in need. That way, when life throws lemons at us, we can make lemonade (which is usually sweeter than lemons), and for each lemon, we turn into lemonade, the world gets a bit better. I need to live with that conviction.

My goal is to write a book about narcissism and psychopathy, which is easy to read. The book may seem narrowly focused on just these two disorders. There are several diagnoses, disorders and addictions that are difficult to deal with and certainly can be as damaging as these.

However, I chose to write about what I encountered the most. I believe that an author's experiences are most important in adding living content to a book. All children who are in need as a consequence of difficulties in their homes deserve society's (thus our) help.

Narcissism and Psychopathy

I am not silent, nor will I ever become silent. That is a very important part of the world I now want to show you. Not to be quiet. I must emphasise this. We all need to make an effort to save as many children as possible of those who now, right now as you are reading this book, are growing up in the tragic home conditions that are created in homes with narcissistic and psychopathic parents.

I don't want to illuminate the perspective of "saving people *from* narcissistic and psychopathic people" alone, but also the perspective of protecting children from ending up in these dysfunctional personalities in the first place. Most people get there for an external reason. In some families, you can follow the disturbances to past unpleasant experiences. So, who is to blame? Should I blame Dad? My grandfather? Grandfather's parents? I cannot spend my time blaming any of them. The only aspect I can influence, and change is my own and my children's future. I am thankful to many circumstances in life for helping me discover that in time.

Living close to people with personality disorders can lead to the fact that we experience psychological poisoning. It can lead to a condition where we no longer tolerate ourselves or know who we are. We lose ourselves. Imagine a work situation where you find yourself strongly affected by a colleague. If we lose all of our self-confidence in that situation, we might collapse completely. When we come across something like this by a parent, it causes serious and permanent damage to a person. Just as flour is kneaded into dough, poison is kneaded into the victim. To collect all the flour (the poison) and throw it away is a task that gets too overwhelming for many people. Even people who manage to detox themselves have a hard time getting rid of all the poison.

Next to the problems we, as a planet, are facing, such as environmental destruction, shortage of resources and many others, this, in my view, is the most important issue. We are living on a poisoned planet, and we allow the destruction of our children by abuse. Some of these children will grow up hurting others, whether animals or people. Children show aggression by acting out for many different reasons. One of them is destructive upbringings.

Human beings are often very self-occupied. At least in our time and in the modern world. So occupied we are that we lack time to stand against injustices and anomalies. Even if we know about a family where something seems to be wrong with the children, we often don't speak for their rights. Perhaps we are happy with our lives, and we do not want any sort of discomfort. This is an unsustainable and dangerous attitude. Do not forget – children raised today are and will remain our children's and grandchildren's future fellows. We spit and swear when someone has been manipulated, deceived, beaten, raped or murdered, but often we are not there to prevent it in the first place.

What we foresee in our collective future is a healthy planet with healthy people. Personality disorders, however, come in the way of this dream of ours. When it comes to personality disorders, people often understand too late that they should have sought some necessary information about it. Not until after encountering the phenomenon do they understand what had happened. They fail to understand that things that might not be visible also exist in the world. I really hope that knowledge increases in the time to come. One to three per cent of all people around the world are expected to suffer from psychopathy, and an even larger number are expected to suffer from narcissism. Do the maths regarding your home country and come up with relevant statistics. With a constant rise in the number of cases of personality disorders, it is very likely that all of us will encounter one or the other at some point in our lives.

Unlike psychopathic individuals, people with a narcissistic personality disorder do have feelings that we, in a way, can understand. At least in the sense that we usually talk about emotions. Psychopathic people are a group that we have learned to hate for hurting others. There is nothing strange about that. However, we cannot ignore the need to study these disorders to be able to prevent them in the future.

Narcissistic people often have been deprived of their childhood and therefore become unable to use emotions in a way that pleases people around them and themselves too. This sometimes ends with them being lonely and bitter, like my dad. His note on the table meant that he hadn't been happy with his life. He had sucked out the rest of us in the family and everything that could have made us genuinely happy to fulfil his ego. It was his will that counted; his matters were the important matters, with him always having a greater say in everything. We, the children in the family, were not built strong because we did not get much attention. He never asked what we wanted to do or if we had any interests. He never tucked us in in the evenings, never asked how our days had been or if we had any homework. In fact, I cannot even remember him saying *'Hi!'* to us when he came home from work.

He made sure that he experienced a lot, yes – A LOT – in his life. He would go on hunting trips to Canada, and he bought a lot of things for himself. In other words, he always did what he wanted. On the other hand, our birthdays did not hold any importance to him.

"One bad chapter does not mean the end of your story."

After all my father did to acquire happiness, he never really experienced happiness. He looked back at his past as a bad chapter. He carried a constant and, of course, painful feeling of emptiness. Neither he himself nor we were able to fill this void from his soul; it was bottomless. Mom tried for over forty years.

When I wrote Safe Harbour, I realised that I lacked something very important. It was true self-esteem. Dad and I both had that devastating flaw to struggle with in our lives. None of us had been helped with self-esteem as children. The development of true self-esteem likely doesn't happen in homes with a narcissistic parent. However, later in life, I managed to work on it successfully after an extensive renovation of myself.

True happiness can only be experienced with some level of self-esteem. Since I believe this so strongly, I centred Safe

Harbour around it. To this day, I'm convinced that it is an essential component of a person's mental life.

During the writing of this book, I have been studying different material on Narcissism and Psychopathy. If you are affected and lack knowledge about these ills, consult books and other sources that are easy to read and contain a summary of the information provided. I suggest this because I understand that you might not have much strength and energy left in your body or soul under their impact. I myself have experienced lots of symptoms after being exposed to this kind of people. As I mentioned - you get poisoned. I know a woman who experienced herself being under so much pressure that her only explanation for starting to lose hair was the stress from living together with a very demanding and very controlling man.

After studying the subject for a rather long time, a big part of my life began to make sense. I understand my life and especially childhood better now. I do have explanations for the problems I have experienced in life. I can't explain how important that has been in formulating my self-image and understanding of the world now. Either there are no words for how much it would mean to my future and, most importantly, to my children and their children.

In the following chapters, I want to briefly show what narcissistic personality disorder means in a research context. Since psychopathy is something that I also encountered, I also want to address that issue. Narcissistic and psychopathic people are not very easy to distinguish by looking at their actions. However, my experience is that a psychopathic person goes a step further than my dad in pleasing themselves; they are "trickier" to put it mildly. There is a difference between the origins of the disorders, and thus different explanations prevail as to why these people are who they are and do what they do. Understanding the background of these individuals is vital in all possible contexts. So that is where we will begin.

Origins of Personality Disorders

Narcissistic and psychopathic individuals have a lot of similarities in their behaviour as compared to ordinary people. However, there are completely different explanations for these behaviours. Psychopathy is also called antisocial personality disorder, but not all antisocial people are psychopathic. It is important to understand this distinction. I, therefore, stick briefly to the concept of psychopathy in this book.

The Narcissistic Person

To begin with, it should be mentioned that there is a kind of narcissism that is called *healthy narcissism*. It is a kind of narcissism of such a "low" level that it helps us to perceive our value, to feel that we are important.

"Healthy narcissism, the investment of energy in one's genuine self, has primitive roots in infancy and early childhood and blossoms into full flower in emotionally, rich, productive and satisfying adult life. It is healthy narcissism that allows us to laugh at ourselves and our imperfection, dig deep within ourselves to create something uniquely ours, and leave a positive personal stamp on the world. Healthy narcissism is the capacity to feel a full range of emotions and share in others' emotional lives, the wisdom to separate truth from fantasy while still being able to dream, and the ability to pursue and enjoy our own accomplishments without crippling self-doubt assertively. It depends on real self-esteem, which is something completely lacking in the people we commonly describe as narcissists." [1]

---

[1] Hotchkiss, S (2008) *Why is it always about you?* The Free Press.

Even though healthy narcissism sounds extremely satisfying, it won't be the focus of our attention in this book. In this book, we will gradually study self-esteem, which I consider to be a more obvious concept, and less confusing than healthy narcissism to gather around. This book, for the most part, addresses narcissism as negative narcissism, one that harms people.

A narcissistic person is in constant fear of not being good enough. The basis of it might be a shattered childhood, where the young child did not receive the necessary support. The child might have had a parent who instilled shame within the child without helping them through their mistakes and without giving sufficient love.

An arrogant and superior attitude serves as a protective barrier that keeps the "stink" of imperfection off the narcissist, providing insulation from intolerable feelings of shame about personal shortcomings. This person gets this attitude from a critical, shaming parent and shame must then be avoided at any cost. So when you encounter arrogance, it's not really pride that you're seeing. Rather, it's a deep and irrational fear of being worthless. The only way they could counter that fear is by feeling important – more important than anyone else [2].

This is, for example, shown by the fact that the person in question doesn't want to achieve mundane goals. They want to perform more magnificent achievements, which they can showcase to the world. Probably they enjoy receiving praise much more than ordinary people do.

Being seen and heard is extremely important, and the narcissistic person wants to stand out from the crowd as an experienced and perfect being. Not just that, they see people who happen to comment or criticise as threats, and from their narcissistic point of view, those people are less intelligent and less valuable. It is difficult for narcissistic people to admit their mistakes and shortcomings. Sometimes, they quit their jobs when they are not allowed to be the best.

There are various theories that have been presented regarding the origin of narcissism. One theory goes that the disorder can arise through congenital disabilities or that it is influenced by genetic inheritance. The researchers who believe that genetic factors influence narcissism, means that

---

[2] Hotchkiss, S (2008) *Why is it always about you?* The Free Press.

some children are more likely than others to become narcissistic [3]. If you as a parent notice traits and behaviours over time that make you suspicious, it is important that you remain attentive and well-read about what to do as a parent.

From my studies, however, I have found a logically accepted theory to explain narcissism. It maintains that a narcissistic person is one whose emotional development has been halted at some point in their early childhood. Long-lasting feelings of neglect, abandonment together with traumatic events, become the causes. It also seems to be caused by unprocessed feelings of guilt and shame. To counter these, the affected use narcissistic traits as a shield. They shut down the sorrow and pain, block their emotions and grow up to eventually become narcissistic.

Shaming the affected child instead of helping them through these feelings adds to the problem. To prevent narcissism in the first place, a parent (and others) needs to show the children love and forgiveness despite their mistake. Not doing that would prove devastating for the child. It dramatically increases the risk of narcissism. The feelings of

---

[3]https://utforskasinnet.se/5-tecken-pa-att-du-uppfostrar-narcissistiska-barn/

shame incited by an individual keep growing within the young person until they become unbearable. The person, therefore, starts "saving themselves" with methods to avoid shame. *Nothing will ever be their fault again.*

A child growing up in a difficult home environment learns what the parents want them to do and how they need to act to avoid the parent's anger for their survival. *"If I do this or say that, mum/dad gets happy or at least not angry…"* Researchers maintain that this may lay the ground for manipulative behaviour that both narcissistic and psychopathic individuals use as a way of life later on.

For a narcissistic person, emotions drive his or her entire life. What these people say is correct, proper and equated with facts. Inside, however, they carry feelings of shame from early childhood, which have now gotten unbearable. They have an emotional immaturity that prevents them from dealing with emotions effectively. So, to cope with the burning shame and the inner critic (often in the forms of others' words from childhood) which constantly degrades them, the narcissistic individuals create an alter ego, or a false self. This is the exact opposite of what the inner critic says they are. But the critic never falls silent [4].

The true self with all the unprocessed emotions is always pressing hard. Therefore, they get stuck in an endless struggle to silence the inner critic and find an outlet for the pressure that is coming from within. Consequently, they blame everything and everyone, push others down, project their emotions, and provoke outbursts to relieve the pressure and prove the inner critic wrong. All they want to do is to prove that the alter ego is their true self. The narcissistic individuals do not let this internal struggle end as that would mean a spiritual death to them. To reach emotional maturity, they would first have to embrace the feelings of shame, acknowledge that their alter ego is false and identify the problems with them. All of this is the exact opposite of what they want to achieve [5].

A narcissistic person does not admit their mental problems. In case of a conflict, it is always others who have issues and never them. They want to feel superior, and it is

---

[4]https://giftigarelationer.com/2017/11/29/skillnad-pa-narcissist-och-psykopat-vad-finns-dar-bakom/
[5]https://giftigarelationer.com/2017/11/29/skillnad-pa-narcissist-och-psykopat-vad-finns-dar-bakom/

imperative for them to always be the best—a person on the top of the world.

Living near narcissistic people often means a lot of stress, as they make others feel less worthy. Everything is welcome if it favours them. All your efforts don't mean anything to them, as they are not even visible. Living together with a narcissistic person implies feelings of inadequacy lasting the entire lifetime. Another thing about narcissistic people is that they can seldom maintain superiority on their own; they use others for that purpose. Someone must be with them in their emptiness in order to keep their image up. Hence, they need others to admire them.

For narcissists, a superior attitude serves as a protective wall that keeps shortcomings out of light. The underlying explanation for this behaviour is that on the emotional level, he or she still is a young child who reacts strongly to unpleasant emotions, especially shame. They are like a two-year-old trapped in an adult body who need people around them to fulfil them. The value of people who surround them is often determined by the benefit they can offer [6].

---

[6] Sigrell, B & Teurnell, L (2011) *Narcissism – jag, mig och mitt*. Lind & Co.

Also, people involved in business or close relationships with those having a narcissistic personality disorder are often taken aback by the extraordinary contradictions of the behaviour they witness. This behaviour is obviously influenced by their selfish needs. These needs are expressed in their demand for constant admiration, underneath which lies an exquisite vulnerability to the slightest rebuff, which ultimately evokes devastating shame [7].

It is important to know that the affected person apparently looks grandiose, boasted, strong and confident. However, on the inside, narcissism is producing self-hatred more than self-love [8]. However, when you meet them and get flattened, it isn't easy to see and accept this fact. At that time, you strongly think of them as unreachable and inaccessible.

My Dad

Shame is a common subject in psychology. There is nothing strange about that because shame is one of the strongest and most painful feelings that human beings can

---

[7] Hotchkiss, S (2008) *Why is it always about you?* The Free Press.
[8] Sigrell, B & Teurnell, L (2011) *Narcissism – jag, mig och mitt.* Lind & Co.

experience. No wonder people blame others for their mistakes and instil shame in them instead.

Like other narcissists, my dad, too, experienced shame. In my presence, he talked about his childhood shame only once. Perhaps he should have talked more about it. It was my grandmother who discussed the subject with me. I wish my dad had dealt with the shame hidden in his heart. In therapy, he could have got help to process the event about the cane and other miseries that happened even earlier in childhood. However, considering that a part of these miseries happened in infancy, they were too early to remember. An example is when his father pulled off his earlobes in frustration. Dad was a child who was screaming from colic...

In the research, they talk about body memories. Traumatic events from one's early childhood can not be remembered consciously. The explanation for this is, according to research, that the brain does not have any language to create memories with at that early stage in life. It is the body that remembers, which learns that other people can not be trusted. One of the most common lessons it internalises is that closeness often *hurts*. Imagine you are lying in your bed having stomach ache until you scream, and then someone close comes to pull your earlobes.

My dad should have processed the memories of abuse he went through in early childhood. He was beaten for events he could not help. Sometimes, he was beaten for things he did not even do. It might not sound strange that you become narcissistic if you are being beaten to become perfect. It might not also be strange that *"nothing EVER was going to be his fault again!"* and that he added a lifelong defence due to a lack of therapy. Interestingly, he mocked the professional group of psychologists and considered therapy ridiculous. The shame probably burned so strongly inside that he almost cried in front of his teenage daughter with his usually strong appearance. He terrorised himself and fought in his own way, I suppose, to be a "better man" outwards than what he really considered himself to be. He oscillated between vulnerability and shame inside and superiority outward towards us.

Unfortunately, he never understood that therapy could have been one of the best solutions to his problems. He denied what he felt and therefore rejected himself. If he had accepted the feelings inside, he might have found it easier not to put everything on our shoulders.

Shame is believed to be the biggest threat to a narcissistic person. Dad's behaviour towards the outside world was, of course, his defence against the severe mental pain shame caused him. He did not only hurt others, but he also prevented himself from developing a genuine self, a true healthy self, and self-esteem. The one who temporarily happens to burst the bubble of perfection for a narcissistic person would most likely become a victim when anger erupts.

I remember an evening when I visited my parents. Dad blamed my boyfriend for things he had not done, and I questioned him because, of course, I wanted everyone to be friends. The relation between my dad and me grew colder than ever, and others told me that dad did not appreciate my moving away from home. I suppose it was very embarrassing to him. I decided to give dad a chance to talk about it but to no avail. What I instead heard was even worse. Maybe he was ashamed again and came up with his most harmful defence. This defence was not at all nice to be exposed to, but I did not have this much knowledge about shame and defence back then as I do now. I could not understand why he became so terribly mean. He did everything he could to put the blame on our shoulders rather than taking the responsibility himself. It was too much of a burden for him. That was my last evening at home. Dad and

I would never be able to become "friends" again; he was inaccessible.

The Psychopathic Person

The psychopathic person, in contrast to a narcissist, lacks an inner emotional life in the sense that we usually talk about emotions. They have no burning shame or inner critics who must be silenced. A psychopathic person is often said to be a copy of a real human being. They mimic emotions but do not experience them as other people do [9].

Rather shockingly, researchers opine that psychopathic individuals can feel empathy, if they choose to, if they have to or if it benefits them. A psychopathic person does not react to his feelings like narcissists do, as they rather seem to be "off."

The underlying motive for a psychopathic person's behaviour is his or her own agenda. These people do things because they feel like it or because it fits into their plan. Many psychopathic people are riskier than narcissists. They seek the kicks in the absence of inner emotional life [10].

---

[9]https://giftigarelationer.com/2017/11/29/skillnad-pa-narcissist-och-psykopat-vad-finns-dar-bakom/
[10]https://giftigarelationer.com/2017/11/29/skillnad-pa-narcissist-och-psykopat-vad-finns-dar-bakom/

Many criminals are psychopathic. It is easy for a psychopathic person to commit crimes for several reasons, such as the following:

- he (usually) or she is not afraid,
- he feels no pity for his victim,
- he is controlled by his impulses and
- he has an easily arousable anger.

Such a person would most likely commit crimes again and again. That is because committing crimes satiate his desires. He gets a kick that nothing else in his life gives him. It is likely that these kicks result in addiction. It is important to clarify that psychopathic individuals do not always commit the crudest of crimes, such as murder or assault. They can be fraudsters in both small and large contexts. Seizing an inheritance or trying to kick you out of your job is not a problem for a psychopathic person [11]. In their interactions with others, a psychopathic person may even receive certain benefits, but they never acknowledge that. They only mention things they have given to others or those

---

[11] Näslund G.K (2004) *Lär känna psykopaten.* Natur och kultur.

they haven't received. This denial of reality puts the people around out of balance.

Researchers have studied blood samples and used magnetic cameras to investigate mass murderers while attempting to find explanations for psychopathic behaviour. The research has shown that there are abnormalities in the brain of these psychopathic individuals, and it is these discrepancies that explain why they lack morality. It is important to be aware of the fact that the most psychopathic individuals are among us looking normal and are not mass murderers.

The fact that there are discrepancies or abnormalities in the brain of psychopathic men and women are now confirmed by an extensive knowledge base. Changed function and structure in parts of the frontal and temporal lobes are linked to violent and antisocial behaviour and psychopathy. We also know from research that mothers' habits can cause psychopathy and other mental disorders to their children during pregnancy, for example by consuming alcohol, smoking, eating poorly or stressing unnaturally. All of these can damage the fetus' brain [12].

Female psychopaths may not be as physically violent as men, but they still demonstrate strange behaviour. They whip up their mood with sudden outbursts and also produce serious lies to seek pity. Sometimes this behaviour is used as a tool to make their way in relationships. In that case, the other will do as she pleases. Such a woman can lie about being pregnant (a very strong "weapon") or might steal important belongings, forcing her partner to come back. She might also threaten to kill them both, maybe by causing a car accident as a consequence of not complying with her demands. A woman like this is often a true Drama Queen, for she magnifies events in her life in a dramatic fashion. She often uses challenging sexuality to lure men into a relationship but then deceives them as the parasitic relationship goes on. This behaviour is referred to as *histrionic personal disorder,* [13] in case you want to learn more about it.

---

[12] Kreis, M, Hoff. H.A, Belfrage, H & Hart, S (2016) *Psykopati.* Studentlitteratur
[13] Rusz, E (2017 Relationspsykopater. Bladh by Bladh

If she is a financial parasite, she can get the victim to sell his home. A time comes when the said person becomes broke while satisfying the psychopathic woman. A psychopathic woman (or man) feels no remorse in exaggerating facts to get damages, charge double compensation, or lying about their income to get financial favours.

Important to Change Perspective

You have been reading very briefly about personality disorders, which is the subject of this book. Some of you might be outrageous after learning about them. If you are a victim, you may be so tired from the abuse that it has become tough for you to stay objective or even care. I believe, however, that this is crucial information, and it is of utmost importance to know the underlying reasons for abnormal behaviour.

For decades, we have had an image of psychopathic people and narcissists as people deserving hatred. Therefore, we possibly ignored the need to learn about the dysfunctional origin of these abominable traits. We must now realise that our hatred has not produced anything useful. It is unfortunate that we lack the knowledge about these disorders to such an extent that we fail to protect ourselves and our close ones from them. We don't know how important it is to confront these problems head-on, and that is why we fail to help people get the right treatment.

The first thing we should do is try to change our understanding and enhance knowledge. I see no progress in this regard if we continue to use the word "psychopath" as a curse. We need to get rid of such degrading terminologies and start looking for explanations for the behaviours so that if we come across children with psychopathic traits, we can treat them in time. Keep in mind that we have to prevent these traits early in life to achieve effective and long-term change.

Research has indicated that it is easier to treat people with psychopathic personality traits in the early years of their life. We need to be very vigilant with the little ones. We have to help them bloom, enable them to live their lives in the best possible manner, despite having a personality disorder. One thing we should teach them is not to harm other humans or animals.

Professor Stephen D. Hart states that psychopathy might be the most important problem that receives the least amount of interest. I want to add that psychopathy is the concept we use the most without really knowing its true means. It gets weird when we call people "psychopaths" without recognising the disorder in real life due to our lack of knowledge and experience.

At this point in time, many children are growing up at the risk of getting a psychological disorder. Some of them will grow up to be extremely dangerous people. Unfortunately, we flee the term psychopathy. Even when we see such traits within a person, we talk secretly about it, not realising how that would contribute to a dangerous world. If we say that *"psychopathy is so unusual, it can't be the problem,"* we will never reach the problem. Nor will we ever get to the problem if we continue to use "Psychopath" as an insult.

It is important to know that narcissism and psychopathy are two of the many possible explanations for antisocial, violent and criminal behaviour. We need the knowledge to understand and see through the surface. We also need to realise that they can't get adequate treatment if people do not get diagnosed in due time. Some researchers believe that psychopathy is deviant antisocial behaviour and not a psychiatric diagnosis. I will not devote space in this book to immerse in that debate about who is right of all the authors and researchers in psychopathy. The focus of this book will be how to ease the problems spreading in the wake of narcissism and psychopathy.

Signs

If you have the checklists of personality disorders, you will realise you could find the signs everywhere. The checklists may be treacherous to use, and they can absolutely not be used to create an understanding of the subject. However, with caution, they can be useful to briefly get an idea of the patterns that occur in a person's behaviour. Being a non-professional, you can't use lists like these to "make diagnoses" out of people's behaviour just when you feel like it. Remember that every antisocial person you meet is not essentially psychopathic or narcissistic but can nevertheless cause you equally serious problems. However, if we are having serious difficulties with a person who might be ruining our lives, these lists may help us discover valuable patterns.

If you know nothing about personality disorders, the narcissistic or psychopathic person can continue to affect your life. You have no chance to defend yourself because you fail to understand what is happening. You might at some point believe that the problem lies within you. The lists of signs of psychopathy and narcissism would help you identify the troublemakers in your life. If you really *are* having problems with a narcissistic or a psychopathic person, the information would hit you like a wall of bricks. Everything would begin to make sense, and you would be relieved to know: *"The problem does not lie within me. I am not wrong. I am not crazy. I am not stupid. Thank god!"*

At the same time, it can be very upsetting to realise that you have been abused in the trickiest way possible. However, bear in mind that it was crucial to find out what has happened and thereby get the chance to understand the phenomenon in greater detail. If I had not seen the first list of narcissistic behaviour, I would not have gotten the opportunity to find out more, to understand better and rescue my life.

According to stats, one to three per cent of ourselves have psychopathy or psychopathic traits. It is not fair if these individuals can go on harming people around them. This can be avoided with the right information so that each of us can analyse situations in our lives ourselves. Self-assessment is also important because individuals who are suffering from personality disorders are unlikely to seek information and help for themselves.

Those who experience abuse at the hands of a person with a personality disorder usually have a hard time persuading both the care system and the legal system to consider their situation. Their main explanation revolves around the manipulative behaviour the perpetrator uses. An outsider would not know who to believe. Everything that the victim says is turned against him or her.

Signs and Symptoms of Narcissistic Personality Disorder

Following are some of the symptoms of a narcissistic person:

- They boast and exaggerate their talents and successes
- They believe they are special or superior to others and require to be treated with great respect
- They need a lot of attention, praise and admiration from others
- They put their own needs first and take advantage of others
- They have difficulties putting themselves into other people's shoes; they lack empathy and regard for others
- They are at first perceived as charismatic and exciting people in their social circle but then turn arrogant and condescending after receiving setbacks

(Jenny Klefbom, psychologist)

Robert Hare's Checklist of Psychopathy Symptoms

- Glib and superficial charm
- Grandiose self-worth
- Need for stimulation or proneness to boredom
- Pathological lying
- Conning and manipulative
- Lack of remorse or guilt
- Shallow affect
- Callousness and lack of empathy
- Parasitic lifestyle
- Poor behavioural controls
- Promiscuous sexual behaviour
- Early behaviour problems
- Lack of realistic long-term goals
- Impulsivity
- Irresponsibility
- Failure to accept responsibility for own actions
- Many short-term relationships
- Juvenile delinquency
- Revocation of condition release
- Criminal versatility

(Robert D. Hare, researcher and pioneer, forensic psychology)

Criticism: This list has been criticised by the author and psychologist Eva Rusz, who argues that not even a serial killer would be classified as a psychopath according to this list. For example, many who abuse their partners have not committed criminal acts in their youth. According to Eva Rusz, these individuals can't be properly diagnosed nor get treated properly. That frees them to abuse their partner for years without risking a diagnosis. They can keep on flying under the radar, as Eva Rusz puts it.

Of course, Professor Robert D. Hare has strong arguments for keeping his list this way. It is clearly about the most violent men. When we talk about victims being abused daily, for example, partners living with psychopathic individuals (both men and women), Eva Rusz places greater reliability on Hervey Cleckley's definition.

Hervey Cleckley's Checklist of Psychopathy Symptoms

- Considerable superficial charm
- Absence of delusions
- Absence of anxiety

- Unreliability, disregard for obligations, no sense of responsibility
- Untruthfulness and insincerity
- Antisocial behaviour
- Inadequately motivated antisocial behaviour
- Poor judgement and failure to learn from experience
- Pathological egocentricity. Total self-centeredness and an incapacity for real love and attachment
- General poverty of deep and lasting emotions
- Lack of any true insight; inability to see oneself as others do
- Ingratitude for any special considerations, kindness and trust
- Fantastic and objectionable behaviour
- No history of genuine suicide attempts
- An impersonal, trivial and poorly integrated sex life
- Failure to have a life plan and to live in an ordered way unless it is for destructive purposes or is a sham.

(Hervey Cleckley, Psychiatrist and pioneer in the field of psychopathy)

There are also bullet lists regarding psychopathic traits in children, CPTI, but these can be found in the chapter about the family and the personality disorder.

Common Traits and Differences

The most common trait of both narcissistic and psychopathic individuals is a distorted and grandiose self-image. Both of them believe they are more important than anyone else. They lack empathy, are manipulative and have a skewed perception of reality. Further, they acquire benefits from others' well-being and do not care about boundaries if it doesn't suit them. Both usually have complicated and problematic relationships. They might be charismatic, charming and act confident, and often attract people with these traits. Both of them are usually admired by their company in the beginning [14].

The men and women I have met, who I strongly suspect of having these personality disorders, did not, of course, appear in the exact same way. Research has shown that there are different types of psychopathic diagnoses. However, based on the bullet lists, I have experienced similarities between those I perceived as having psychopathic traits and those like my dad – narcissists. My experience reveals that psychopathic individuals stick out when it comes to their

---

[14]https://giftigarelationer.com/2017/11/29/skillnad-pa-narcissist-och-psykopat-vad-finns-dar-bakom/

ability to frame people. This they manage to do by being manipulative, lying and by being unbelievably fraudulent. They make a mess that nobody, in the end, can understand even when they consciously try to. The psychopathic individuals hide and lurk. They jerk and pull a little here, a little there, so everything ends with absolute confusion on all fronts. I am very grateful that my dad did not act that way. A person can be narcissistic without being psychopathic, but seldom the other way around. A psychopathic person usually has a narcissistic personality disorder, too [15].

Of all people I have met and who I firmly believe have problems of this kind, I will never receive answers regarding who is suffering from what. Why? Because, of course, they will never participate in such research and get diagnosed. Usually, people like this do not seek help concerning their flaws in life. It is important to clarify that just because a person has one or two traits matching with those on the checklists, it does not mean they are suffering from a personality disorder. There are mentally healthy people who lack morality whenever they feel it suits them, i.e. without being psychopathic. Of course, people can also be

---

[15] Rusz, E (2017 Relationspsykopater. Bladh by Bladh.

psychopathic to various extents and behave differently from others of their kind. On the other hand, if you feel most of the points in the checklist characterises the person that torments you – your assessment is probably right.

When things in your life get seriously wrong or rather strange involving a specific person with a personality disorder, it is very important to have knowledge. Only knowledge would help you to deal with them. You already know that these people are experts in getting what they want, and it will be you sacrificing everything for them if you lack knowledge or understanding of their behaviour. In one of the reference books, you can read about a narcissistic mother who all of her life played nasty with her children to get her way. She was even happy to have broken her leg to retain control over her adult children. Now imagine how important it is for you to be cognizant of such behaviour.

A narcissistic person also starves people around them for putting efforts in a relationship, so when they suddenly make an effort, you believe that everything is fine and that you have been wrong about them all this time. The truth is that they do the bare minimum for others and get maximum benefits in return. They would fool you to trust in them and invest in them, over and over again.

Do You Smell a Rat?

Don't Jump to Conclusions…

Maybe at this point, you are smelling a rat regarding somebody you know. Wait, do not jump to conclusions. Do not start calling people narcissists and psychopaths whenever you feel like it. That is an important part of this whole thing. Do not generalise, do not use these words for other people when you might just not like them for yourself. You may simply just have met a person with a hot temper, lack of morality or a person with a big ego, but that does not mean you tag them with a narcissist or psychopathic label. Stay as objective as you can.

But Don't Wait for Too Long Either

After reading the previous chapter thoroughly and objectively recalling the experiences involving a particular person, you will begin to feel if they are suffering from a personality disorder or from some other serious diagnosis. It is felt throughout your body. The person in question has crawled inside your skin. You feel poisoned; you feel extremely week and worthless. Do not let it go that far.

I have been unfortunate to meet a number of such people. I am so sure about it that I can outright say it. Sometimes I would become angry with myself afterwards for taking such a long time to realise and see through things. The mildest way to put it is that the diagnosis is "tricky." In my case, for instance, when I come across these characteristics in a new person, in another context or in a new place, I simply do not understand it in time; it takes me a while to comprehend what's really going on.

I see every new person I meet through a completely fresh perspective, and I guess that is what we all ought to do. We tend to believe in people. Unfortunately, every time they managed to harm me before I could discover the illness in them. Every time, they attacked and injured my self-esteem. Recovering from such an experience is no easy feat. It usually takes a long time to retrieve peace of mind after being attacked so brutally. Perhaps, some memories from those experiences would stay in my mind forever.

How Can We Influence and Change?

One of my dreams in life is to employ this difficult matter for the better. I strongly believe that this problem will grow if we do not pay attention. We need to discover psychopathic and narcissistic patterns in families where bad things are going on. It is not uncommon for children to grow up to be like their parents. Learning more on this subject can help children as even children sometimes develop psychopathic traits during childhood. It is a challenging but essential task that society and ourselves must undertake in this regard (by the way – WE are the society).

One good thing is that there is growing awareness on this subject. Suppose the affected people get hold of the kind of literature, such as the one I am writing right now, where the personality disorders are noticed, or they come across something written on the internet that hits them. In that case, they might try to find a way out of the predicament themselves. We all need to help one another by spreading knowledge about these difficult things so that somebody's illness can be diagnosed in time.

You who get this information – do not be silent. I hope from my heart that people will talk to each other about life's difficulties. If they are lucky, they might meet somebody who understands what's going on. Maybe they are affected by a person with a personality disorder or are having a child who is at risk. The fact that we are so many around the world who pay attention and also spread knowledge speaks volumes for what we can do to make this world better. On your individual level, help people who need you within the family. From the outside, it is often difficult to discover. As

I wrote earlier: Not even a person with my misfortune of running into these people discover the traits until after the damage has been done. We would not be having any problems with it if it was easy.

Experiences of the Psychopathic Traits

When you meet a person with psychopathy or with psychopathic traits, your world will soon be turned upside down. Probably you will be the one who needs to act for a change at home, school or workplace. It is difficult, not to say impossible, to "win" against people like this, as they act so cunningly, and nobody can imagine that a psychopathic person might be in their vicinity. But really, it is no utopia if there is. One to three per cent of the population is said to be suffering from psychopathy. Even a bigger number is suffering from narcissism. It is most likely that all of us will encounter one of them sooner or later.

Psychopathy is something that many people wish not to talk about. If it continues on that road, those people can keep on ravaging quite freely. Now, let us go through some of the experiences with psychopathic individuals.

Oh, Such an Amazing Person!

A person with psychopathic traits knows how to get accepted, and more than that. They make you feel as if you have met the perfect man or woman in the world! You instantly feel that this is a person you would like to spend time with, or this is a person who could become a major part of your life, in the capacity of a partner, friend or colleague.

But after a while, especially if the person doesn't get his or her way, the misery begins. You, on your behalf, are having difficulties adjusting to the new situation. You, the mentally healthy person, are firmly settled with the belief that this is such an amazing man or woman. Absolutely amazing! It will take some time for you to change your views regarding this person. Inside your head, you come up with a lot of excuses for their changed behaviour. You think maybe your partner, friend or colleague is just having a bad period, feels bad about something, is stressed or concerned regarding his or her children, or having PMS, and the list goes on.

Yes, I Can Line Up!

Psychopathic people can soon turn out to be completely impossible to work with. They can not / do not want to meet anyone halfway. They don't want to give, just take. You can get the feeling that you must drop your own needs and sacrifice your own life for him or her. You have to line up or be there all the time. If they don't get what they want, they will cause problems for you, or they will choose to ignore you. You may have been extremely accommodating. You may have sacrificed to such an extent that you feel offended, but the person in question still demands more. You feel compelled to help, to line up! Besides, you're the only one trying to solve the problems.

I Give, and I Give, and I Give

Psychopathic people will not withdraw the least from lying to others and benefit from that, preferably at the expense of others. If they want something, they'll take it. And probably they will never get enough of it. They cherry-pick the rewards for themselves, and you will get the left-overs, especially if the left-overs are rotten. They can call you and, with calculation, turn things over, make a mess in your head, in a way that you don't understand how you agreed to things you didn't want. Even if you understand you agree to something you don't want, you lack the strength to fight back.

Then, all of a sudden, the said person makes a positive gesture. You immediately think that you may have been wrong about him or her. You feel guilty because you, *despite everything*, may have judged your friend too fast. When it has gone this far, you are so used to doing everything, to agreeing with everything, you have been exploited so many times that now minimum effort from the psychopathic person will be amount to unreasonable proportions. And you keep giving and giving and giving.

Why So Angry with Me? Please Let Me Explain!

Have you ever sent a text message to which you didn't get an answer right away? Have you in that situation thought: Hm…. strange… is she angry with me? That may be enough to make you feel uneasy. The silence when you desperately expect an answer can be unbearable.

A person with psychopathic traits may be a skilled user of passive-aggressive behaviour. You notice that the person seems angry with you. You don't know what you might have done to cause this reaction, so you ask directly, but you don't get an answer. You ask again. No answer. Instead of answering, the person walks away, snorts, raises eyebrows or pretends that he or she is very, very busy. Yes, he or she shows conveys that you are worthless. Totally worthless.

If you are accused of something, which you didn't do or didn't mean, you want to declare yourself innocent, right? You try repeatedly, but you will never get the chance to explain or defend yourself. A psychopathic person makes sure to jump right on to the next subject or respond with silence. You may notice that you become more and more desperate to reach out to the person, but it only leads you to become more and more devastated every day.

Even if this has happened to me repeatedly, the person gets to me every time. I have always been a person who finds flaws within myself instead of others. So instead of the narcissist perspective "nothing is my fault," my perspective in life has been "everything might be my fault." Growing up in a narcissistic family made me that way. This also made me a magnet for that kind of people. Some children from these families become narcissistic themselves, an important issue discussed in this book. But it is also important to mention the children growing up to be the opposite.

Maybe you're a person like me, the opposite, who also have worked hard to build self-esteem. These personality types, however, will demolish your self-esteem in no time. You feel like you are the worst person in the world. The narcissistic person wants you to crawl. He or she tries to turn everything around and make himself or herself seem like the victim, make you feel ashamed of something you did without knowing what you did wrong. And he or she will manage to do this to you. You will run after the person and ask and ask. If you come up with something that you believe might be the reason for such behaviour, you ask him or her, Is it this? Is it that? The person still won't answer, and finally – you crawl. You, who are healthy, have become so desperate to find out what you did wrong that you won't relax, unwind, or forget about it. The psychopathic person eats you from the inside and knows it.

It is probably the case that the person has not received his or her way to the level of 100 % to 110 %. Psychopathic individuals are easily offended in these situations. If you don't know anything about this kind of psychological torture already, then you won't understand it. You will be totally wing broken when the "penalty period," maybe, or probably not, is over. However, the next time you fail to satisfy the psychopathic person, it starts all over again.

Is He Lying?

Lying, as previously mentioned, is not a problem for a psychopathic person. To them, every lie is okay if it leads to benefits. If they need to lie to get their way, it's just fine, according to them. They may tell very serious lies which affect hundreds of people. Maybe even millions of people, depending on who the person is. Nothing is allowed to stand in the way when he or she wants something. It may seem surprising, but it's no big deal to get revealed either. It's simply not a big deal.

A lie can, for example, be used to skip a job, a job that didn't seem attractive to go through with. It will be others who work instead of them, but of course, that doesn't matter. They still don't care about others.

Finally, after several lies, you start to wonder if this person really is truthful. Suddenly someone has discovered from social media that the current person was not ill at all. Instead, it might have been a nice trip or an errand that needed to be done. Ignoring work doesn't mean that you won't get your salary. No, there's nothing wrong with ignoring to report sickness or taking time off without telling anyone at the finance department. Getting paid without having to work is obviously no problem!

Sometimes the problems grow even bigger. Much bigger. People may be offered benefits to agree to the disordered persons will. Sometimes, people are provided benefits to keep quiet. This results in the ugliest of the ugliest world for normal people.

The Money

Several of the people I have met, who I suspect are having a personality disorder, have had an unhealthy view of money. They don't seem to reach financial balance, and if we look back at the checklists regarding psychopathic personality, we understand why. Wasting money is not always the problem; it can be greed too. But why is a human greedy? Well, probably to save money for him or herself. They want to be able to invest one hundred per cent in themselves.

Sometimes I have noticed that they seem to see themselves as victims in order to justify their behaviour. An example might be that they take one or two extra sacks of soil from the garden store in springtime and justify it by saying, "It's so expensive anyway." So, in this situation, they are victims of stores taking their money. A person with a personality disorder may most likely ask to borrow money from you or ask you to get something from the store, but you will never see your money again. He or she can also participate in a project, but when the project is completed, and the bill arrives, they're no longer interested. They may come up with excuses such as the project didn't work out as they expected. They may have great demands but are not prepared to sacrifice.

I'm a Lousy Person! I Feel Sick!

If personality disordered people are losing a discussion, they'll start offending you. He or she may suddenly become very angry. Angry in a way that makes you scared or at least very uncomfortable. They allow themselves to be "sharp," unpleasant, angry and threatening, but if you only once get provoked to an outburst, you will be seen as an uncontrolled nervous wreck, and people around you will be told what you are! A greedy person with a personality disorder turns things around so you will look like the greedy one. They act like that with every unfavourable trait they have. Turn it over so that it would be transferred to you.

If you are winning a discussion and they don't know what to answer, they can also say: "Yes, always knows best, you always know best." A perfect phrase if you want to reduce another person's importance and worth. There is no limit to how sarcastic these people may sound with their tone and with their words. Finally, you will feel like a lousy person. Totally worthless, really.

To succeed in overcoming you, these people control you with such cruel grips that you are forced to give up on your stance. They use a number of master suppression techniques. The false accusations, the silence, the violations and the threats will haunt you for a long time after being exposed. They keep going until they get what they want and affect you to such an extent that you will get poisoned and become ill unless you manage to get out of their claws and go away from them.

What Happened? I've Probably Gone Crazy...

People with personality disorders are most likely experts on giving you a bad conscience. A narcissistic individual has a very immature emotional life. Psychopathic individuals have no emotional side at all unless it benefits them, it is said. If one of them can't come home to you right now, while you may be busy, they probably won't come at all, or they will push themselves through your door. You are the one who'd have to adapt to their wishes.

It is almost impossible to speak substantially with these people. They just can't see things that are obvious and correct in other people's eyes if they don't benefit them. I have experienced that they can't be objective if what is said doesn't suit them and gets in the way of their plans. I have on several occasions witnessed their rejection concerning objective people who don't give in, simply because they are wise and know for a fact that they are right. That means a risk to their plans and rampaging, and that, of course, is strongly disliked.

Maybe you'll wake up one day and start wondering why you feel so terribly bad, and maybe you begin to analyse the situation. If you haven't encountered this before or even heard of it, you might not understand even now. You just feel sick and sad about the fact that you've made so many mistakes lately. You've lost control, and you think that you may have gone crazy. You, who are reading this book, may at this point think, *"How can a person let it go so far? I would have understood this earlier..."* But this is what's special with this type of people. They know how to break you down. It's on their agenda to keep you from understanding, but you won't know that. Purpose number one is to make you believe that it's you who are "wrong" in every way. Purpose number two, to get what they want.

The Chessboard

Usually, I use the analogy of a *chessboard* to my closest friends, and they get the hint. On a chessboard, you figure out which pieces you can use to knock out as many opponent pieces as possible. Just as in a chess game, knocking out other people in real-life situations is a psychopathic person's great arena. In real life, he or she is the king or queen. A psychologically healthy person would never be able to figure out all these moves to get rid of all the others, and sometimes also how to do it in a surprisingly short amount of time. On the chessboard, the psychopathic person chooses which ones should be allowed to participate further and which ones shouldn't. The ones who are allowed to participate are, of course, the ones who won't be standing in the way of the plans of getting what he or she wants.

Suddenly, the people around you begin to change their stories. What they said yesterday no longer applies. Someone, it may be unclear who, has made them change their statements. You now face a completely unreliable world. Your sense of safety is blown away. If you point something out concerning the current person, you must have proof. In the human resource department, they ask for recordings, which can prove what you claim, but you have never thought of recording or take notes.

If you have a psychopathic boss, he may try to make you sign important, rather crucial documents. Do not do it! If a psychopathic person doesn't win a negotiation or discussion in the workplace, they may go ahead and manipulate their way up to the top. He or she may, for example, get management to be suspicious of the employees who don't suit them. They may distort most statements that the employees have said to twist the meaning and damage their reputation. In other words, they manipulate information. Lying about other people is no problem for them, nor to put you up against a third person, if it benefits them, or keeping important information away from you so you will look like a fool… None of your commonly heard arguments seems to work. Just a minute ago, you were a highly respected and well-liked person in the workplace…

In such a situation, if you notice that a colleague is exposed to this person as well, there is a risk of that being used by the psychopathic person. It is a conspiracy! It is you who have come together, and you are the evil ones. Two against one! That's not fair! All you say to defend yourself will be used to make him or herself seem like a victim. You will not be trusted in what you say, and the more you stand up for yourselves, the more you assert that you're telling the truth, the more it will lead you to lose trustworthiness in the eyes of people. It's still you who are the evil, and now it's time for you to calm down!

You may realise in the situation that you have been exposed to a "cat and mouse game." If you don't realise, you will most certainly walk away with a big dent in your self-esteem, your whole person. You have been attacked.

The worst thing, in my opinion, isn't the pain of being exposed. The worst of the worst, the most devastating feeling of all, which make you feel that you cannot bear your coming days, is *not being believed*. That is a terrible thing, which makes a person almost lose their footing after a long period of torment. You and the people around you have been lied to, been manipulated, and you have been treated with emotional coldness. In the worst scenario, *you* will be the evil one in the manager's perspective, as a consequence of you not being believed at all. In the "best" scenario possible in this situation, the concepts of *manipulation, lying,* and *emotional coldness* by the manager would be exchanged with *misunderstandings, difficulties in communication* and *difficulties in cooperation with others*. That way, you "only" need to take on half the blame. Furthermore, the fact that you need to take on half the blame would eat you from the inside because you know it's not what happened. You know it isn't right.

After being exposed, you may get stuck in your own thoughts for a while, hyper-thinking, flashbacks… If you do come from a narcissistic home or a home with a psychopathic family member, this may cause trauma within you.

Since I have met a few of these people myself, I must say I've become very tired of being affected by them. They have a twisted perception of reality, and it is exhausting to keep on adapting to them. A life without them, though, is probably impossible to perceive. However, for everyone and each of them that I've met, I've noticed that I get less affected psychologically. I think that is because I so very well know how they operate, and I know it has *absolutely nothing* to do with me. At the time when I was not aware, it was really devastating. The nature of the problem is such that the innocent is to take on the blame. *But it really has nothing to do with me; the problem is the disorder.*

If I recognise the chessboard, *I know* and *understand* what's going on – do I then dare to put my foot down? In fact, nowadays, I have begun to see through this behaviour. It may still take a while, but eventually, I see it. I know I'm walking into a minefield. If I take the step to accuse another person of being a psychopath, narcissist, unreasonable or deceptive or maybe not completely healthy, I risk being considered unreasonable, extremely accusatory, irrational, and tense in my assessment. Yes, I may even be a crazy person. Maybe I am the one lacking the perception of reality? Maybe it is the psychopathic person who is the victim? It may even be me who is wicked… Right there, I have given the psychopathic person exactly what he or she needs. The disadvantageous traits that this person has, those qualities will be attributed to me. Then I know how I will be perceived, don't I?

Sometimes I have been wondering if a psychopathic person thinks it's a positive thing to be offended. This is because it gives him or her the ticket to striking back a thousand times. There are no limits to what they then can invent, and it is excused with *"the thing that happened before."*

I am aware of the fact that a psychopathic person can infect an entire workplace to such an extent that the management all the way to the top loses its grip, fires the decent employees, starts lying to cover up their mistakes and offend others in the staff group in desperation to get the situation under control. If or when they discover the chessboard and its king or queen, the staff may have decreased considerably. Unfortunately, the wrong people may have left. The advice you often get is, in fact, to leave because you can never win. You also cannot bear to weather the storm. It's not worth it for the sake of your health. Sometimes I have said, "It takes a fool to remain sane, and I'm no fool." The strain of relating to narcissistic and psychopathic people is far too great.

Everyone has to make their own decision whether to tell their story or not. As I said, it can be difficult to "win." Unfortunately, my experience at this point is solid. To make the best of a bad situation, I will, with great confidence, take my book under my arm and let the words flow. I don't have to win, but no one should ever silence me.

Again: They Are Not Happy

What makes my life worth living is the love I give and receive, the empathy I feel towards the living around me, creating sustainability, taking a pause and feeling happiness - the enjoyment of the sunshine in April and feeling reverence for nature.

Everything I believe makes my life worth living is probably lacking within people with narcissistic or/and psychopathic personality disorder. In the beginning, I mentioned that I sometimes want to call many of them personality destroyed instead of disordered. Many of them probably grew up in an environment which made them this way. Of course, they are victims too. Most likely, they suffer as a consequence of their inadequacies, even though it is well known that some of these people might not experience emotions in a way that we can understand. There are researchers who mean that the situation is not as hopeless as we believe when it comes to psychopathic individuals and their capacity to experience emotions. There is more about that later in the book. One thing that interests me is the fact that psychopathic people are said to be narcissistic as well, but not necessarily the other way around. We know that narcissistic people do experience feelings in a sense that we, in a way, can understand.

A common perception about psychopathic people is that their only purpose is to harm other people and that it is revenge for a cracked childhood. But I also think that sometimes it might be the fact that they desperately try to get what they want and hurt others to get it at all costs. Afterwards, they don't find it within themselves to repair the damage if it doesn't help them to further get what they want. The purpose itself might not be to hurt others, but if people get hurt on their way to the goal, they don't care. Apologising is something they just aren't able to. They may try to smooth it over, but they won't apologise.

What they need to realise is that their behaviour doesn't benefit them in the long term. They make so many bad decisions that, in the long run, they won't be able to find peace anywhere with anyone. They might not find a partner or a job without moving far away, where bad reputation won't follow them. They know what they want, and they want it *now*. All the time, they want things *now*. They can't wait for gratification – this is a problem that leads to grave consequences for them in life. That way, it becomes impossible to keep stability in life.

The psychopathic person (and the narcissistic too, for that matter) can get into serious trouble when he or she has been revealed and therefore also has irritated a large crowd of people, for example, at a workplace. There are completely obvious shortcomings associated with such behaviour, and there can also be evidence presented, but the disordered personality is unable to bend regardless. He or she cannot accept the fact that the mistakes are theirs. It's everyone else's fault; everybody else is wrong. Everyone else is whiny or unintelligent, or they are lying.

This might result in several and completely absurd discussions while the disordered person is considering himself the victim of other people's cruelty and evilness. Narcissistic individuals become victims because they are unable to accept that they made a mistake, or two, or three mistakes. It is a devastating defect in the long run. Against a big crowd, even a narcissistic person stands no chance. From the perspective of the narcissist, it is a wolf-pack coming to throw themselves over him - the innocent victim.

With age, it also happens that a narcissistic person becomes more and more anxious to get approval from others in order to retain prestige. This is because he or she somehow feels that the "glory days as young, strong, successful and beautiful" are over. There are people who see this through and take advantage of it. They may not have any feelings for the disordered personality, and therefore, they don't care about him or her. When these people discover how much a little flattery can do for the narcissistic elderly person, understand that this is an addiction, they begin to deceive. For example, a narcissistic person might have difficulties admitting that he doesn't have a lot of money, so it is difficult to refuse when others try to buy things from him cheaply or invite themselves to a fancy dinner with alcohol. That means that the narcissistic person oneself runs a risk of becoming an exploited victim by people who see through this total lack of true self-esteem.

Now, you have read examples of how these people can be and how they might act. My heart always goes back to the children. None of the narcissistic or psychopathic individuals can possibly be genuinely happy with their lives. Of course, our strongest wish is for children to grow up to be healthy and happy adults. Growing up in narcissistic or psychopathic homes won't benefit them. Not at all.

- The narcissistic person struggles with an alter-ego because of a broken childhood. Imagine my dad's childhood. Such horror! Seeing his mother get beaten up, knowing that she hid in the forest during the night. To get abused himself. Live in constant fear of what will happen and therefore watch every little step you may take. And every family member's steps as well. To get terrified if you happen to make a mistake – Cause *"what will happen if dad sees it?"* I know that my grandmother with a rug hid a mark that my dad accidentally made on the floor. She was terrified because she knew that dad would be at risk if my grandfather saw it.

- The psychopathic person lacks emotional qualities, which leads to difficulties with all kinds of human relations. The moral-compass was never created – or in some cases – it was destroyed along the road. Hervey Cleckley, as previously mentioned, is a psychiatrist who has strongly influenced the thinking regarding psychopathy. In his book, The Mask of Sanity, he meant that psychopathy probably could be explained by a biological defect in the brain. He had seen far too many psychopathic people growing up in what appeared to be normal families. Now there is evidence for his hypothesis. Structural brain differences, brain defects. "Psychopaths" (I don't really like the word) are a highly disliked group of people. No wonder about that, considering their acts, but sometimes such behaviour is a result of a defect in the brain that never was detected. In some cases, it happens due to being abused as children. Psychopathy can occur through injuries /structural brain defects, but childhood trauma can also cause the disorder [16]. In these cases, it would be

---

[16] P3 Relationsradion, Karolina Sörman – Forskare Psykopati vid Karolinska institutet.

correct to call them 'personality destroyed' to get an active approach to personality disorders instead of a passive one.

Although there is evidence for structural brain defects causing psychopathy, the disorder cannot be said to be congenital. The explanation for this fact is that all people with these structural brain defects do not develop psychopathy - a favourable childhood matters. As previously mentioned, alcohol or drug abuse by pregnant women might cause psychopathy within their children. The environment in which these children grow up can be of crucial importance. An alcohol-abusing mother who is allowed to keep her child is no solution. To begin with, she should have spent all her pregnancy in a rehabilitation clinic.

The childhood environment will be absolutely crucial to these children. There are people with structural brain defects or damaged brain areas who grow up to be functional adults. A good upbringing environment may be the answer to this mystery. A good upbringing environment doesn't exist in a home with alcohol abuse.

If a psychopathic person behaves selfishly most of the time, for example, towards relatives or colleagues, he or she will not succeed in the long run. But there are hopes:

A statement by a female with structural brain defects as in psychopathy: *"If I notice the others feel different, I can tell them: 'Okay, I don't feel that way, but I know you normal people do, so let's do it your way'."* She manages her life with the knowledge that she isn't like everybody else and that she is different. To make her life work, she adapts to the fact that she suffers from a disorder. I believe this woman grew up in a home with stability, love and understanding. Things are going well, and by making the social life work, she is, of course, able to use her capacity and skills in a good way. From her home, she has probably, from an early age, learned the difference between right and wrong and also had a predictable home environment as support. Through this, she has got a chance to function well in society. She is no mean person; she just doesn't interpret feelings in the same way others do. That way, she can still be a happy person in her own way.

If, on the other hand, a child grows up with a psychopathic person as a caretaker and role model and takes an impression from his or her manipulative personality, the child might seem to have or, in fact, develop psychopathic traits without starting life with structural brain defects. It is then caused by the environment. Within this lies hope. But not if we close our eyes to the knowledge that exists. Not if it continues to be completely impossible to detect or suspect personality disorders. Nor if we let children stay in these extremely destructive environments.

As I write this book, my feelings vary between sadness and anger. At first, sadness hits, then anger and then sadness again. You naturally feel anger when you hear about, or encounter, the disordered people that are hurting others. Within him or her, however, is probably in many cases, a child who was once let down. A child who didn't get a good start in life. They have not been helped by people around them, people who have been tiptoeing or closing their eyes.

Everywhere you can read that escaping from a psychopathic person is the right thing to do. I agree. Adults often have a choice and the possibility to do so. A child is stuck, doomed to stay with a dysfunctional parent. We must protect the children, and it is our job as stable adults, with the purpose to not let them become another dysfunctional generation of parents.

The more knowledge we gain about these disorders, we understand that the personality disordered people is a group that, due to poor growing up conditions or biological defects that have been ignored, may end their lives alone. They will have to move if they want to come close to people because rumours are spreading in their social surroundings. The more aware people around them become, the faster the disordered individuals will be revealed. It may not be such a bright prospect for them, but them being revealed is the only way if there should be even the slightest chance to help them as adults. Yes, I snort too when I see what I'm writing. They don't want any help, and they don't even realise that there is something wrong with them.

However, there are experts who say that it is possible to help them towards awareness, even in adulthood. Let's avoid witch-hunting, but they really need to come to light. That way, there may be hope. Psychopathic lonely wolves sometimes become the most dangerous of people. As long as it is possible to fly under the radar, they will probably never change. Without their experience telling them that the harmful and fraudulent behaviour doesn't benefit them, they will never stand a chance to get a functional life.

In their perspective, their behaviour benefits them, and an awakening concerning themselves is therefore not needed. If they get away with every bad action they make, we can as well tell them that their behaviour is a possible way to lead their lives.

There are amazing people who dedicate their lives to counteract this problem. Those are people with an aptitude to reach the most difficult personalities and diagnose them. If the personality disorder has involved more problems than 'joy' in the psychopathic, or more likely the narcissistic person's life, we can't really know how every one of them would react to get their disorder revealed. One small part of them might get curious about treatment. We should never say never.

The Family and the Personality Disorder

Psychopathy

The issue of heredity and environment is of great importance regarding psychopathy. Worldwide research tells us that inheritance does matter in determining psychopathic traits. However, the extent of these traits being reflected in a person's adult personality often depends on upbringing. Hence, how the child is treated while growing up becomes an important concern.

A good upbringing, with good role models and a loving environment, shows a great positive impact on the psyche of the children. This may be totally crucial for the child's future.

According to researchers, psychopathic personality traits can be seen as early as the age of three, even earlier according to other researchers. Still, the debut is often set from six to ten years of age.

Many grown-up children have told us about how they grew up in an environment where they didn't know how the mood would change from one second to the next. The father could, in one moment, abuse the mother, and the next moment everything was "just fine." This, of course, gave them an incredibly insecure environhent to grow up in. Really devastating.

When the child grows up and becomes more independent, the parents and the home environment have a lesser influence on them. Instead, friends have a more influential role. There are studies that show that the structure and function of the brain can change when our mindset and behaviour change. Helping children and young people from destructive backgrounds can be crucial to their future [17]. They need to experience a healthy and predictable world.

Narcissism

"Narcissism is a normal stage we all pass through in early childhood on our way to becoming more complete human beings. To make the transition, we need the help of healthy parents who have their own unhealthy narcissism in reasonable check and are capable of nurturing individuality in their children while teaching values and respect for others. When parents are themselves narcissistic, they often use their children in self-serving ways and fail to guide them to a healthy resolution of normal childhood narcissism. The

---

[17] Kreis, M, Hoff. H.A, Belfrage, H & Hart, S (2016) *Psykopati.* Studentlitteratur.

result is another generation of narcissists – as well as people who seem to be magnets for this personality type." [18]

Narcissistic parents thus also raise children with an opposite personality to narcissism, susceptible to shame and insecurity in their personal relationships and therefore attract narcissistic or psychopathic personalities [19].

The Opposite of Narcissism

In the world of narcissism, the one who should be ashamed is not. They turn it over, so their victim is ashamed instead. The narcissistic person makes the victim bend to his or her will because they themselves are not capable of adapting. A top position on the podium is required, and everyone else has to stand in the lower positions.

In my family, I was crushed time and again. As a result of this, I have grown into an extremely sensitive person when it comes to moods. I am sensitive to the will of others and have been feeling insecure among people for a long period of my life. In 2012, I wrote about my journey from nobody to somebody. I didn't yet know that I, just like my

---

[18] Hotchkiss, S (2008) *Why is it always about you?* The Free Press.
[19] Hotchkiss, S (2008) *Why is it always about you?* The Free Press.

dad, had grown up in narcissistic families. I'm amazed when I study facts about the narcissist's children because it's about me, who became a sensitive person, extremely susceptible to shame, and it is also about my dad, who became like his father. The only difference, but a crucial one, of course, was that my grandfather was physically violent to a larger extent. Otherwise, they acted quite in the same way.

Even though I'm very conscious nowadays, I can still be sensitive to people who want confirmation in a narcissistic way. What I must do then is to stop and analyse the situation and try to understand what's really going on so that I'm not getting dragged down by old habit. Furthermore, I am very sensitive to other people's irritation and anger. That is not only a bad thing, but sometimes I believe that people might get angry when they're not. This triggers my former feelings of insecurity, and therefore it is important to seek help to unlearn and re-learn. In the same vein, one should learn to interpret signals correctly because triggers make you go back in time; it's trauma speaking.

When I encounter people with a tough appearance, and if they cross the line of what is okay to say, I keep my distance. An example might be when a woman, without any shame, said: *"I will never get a great deal of money because*

I have no rich relative to wish dead." I feel the energy very strongly around people that I experience as being tough, you know - in a bad way. Of course, I can be near them when I must, but they may gladly stay on my doorstep.

When growing up in a narcissistic home, it is sometimes also difficult to keep the balance in life. Don't be *too much* but don't be *too little*, is the ongoing mantra.

Following is the voice which comes from <u>feeling</u>: *Don't talk too much, people won't like you if you do. Don't take up too large space; people won't like you if you do. Don't write too many e-mails; people won't like you if you do. Don't drive too slow; people won't like you if you do.*

In the other ear, there is another voice, the voice which comes from <u>learning</u>: *You have the right to speak until you feel that you are finished. You have as much right to be here as anybody else. If you need to write a larger number of e-mails to receive answers to your questions, you ought to do it. You have the same rights as everyone else to use this road, and you also have the right to drive a bit slower than the others if you feel like it.*

Still, driving on that damn road, you will hear the voice whispering in your ear:

They may not like you; they may get irritated; they may honk the horn for you to get out of their way.

This is a horrible position to put someone in. It is an exhausting way to live.

Another way growing up in a narcissistic family has affected me is when people in a discussion don't stick to the point but instead become genuinely evil; forty years of memories wash over me. This feeling, the sensitivity to aggression, affects me in writing too. For example, I find it very strenuous to read a text in which there are many exclamation marks. To me, it looks aggressive, as long as it isn't positive exclamations, of course. The content of this book really gives reasons for many exclamation marks, but you have to look to find them. It is important to me to write as calm texts as possible. To be exposed in childhood really affects the whole person.

Post Narcissist Stress Disorder

"Trauma is personal. It does not disappear if it's not validated. When it is ignored or invalidated, the silent screams continue internally heard only by the one held captive."

Danielle Bernock

Before moving on to the problems within narcissistic families, I want us to take a close look at the diagnosis victims may suffer from after being exposed:

I know that I've been suffering from PNSD, *Post Narcissistic Stress Disorder*. Now, many people may ask themselves: *What is that? Does she mean PTSD (Post Traumatic Stress Disorder)?*

My answer to that question is: *No, I don't mean PTSD; I mean PNSD, even if the symptoms are much the same.*

A few years ago, my PNSD got worse. Me telling you about nervousness driving a car, and avoiding speaking too much, also not writing too many emails… That's about PNSD. My curator said that I probably suffered from PTSD, and she needed to write a referral for me to see a psychologist educated enough to handle this sort of diagnosis. She wanted us to write this referral together. I told her that we probably needed to write that I grew up in a narcissistic home. However, since she wasn't comfortable using such a word, she didn't. Instead, the referral came in with the suspected diagnosis of Post Traumatic Stress Disorder.

A few weeks later, my curator received a document in which the psychologist asked for more details. He wanted to know more about the traumatic event I had encountered. She immediately realised that there was nothing to write. There was no *single traumatic event* to be found in my life. She knew, though, that this was about my *whole life*. When she laid eyes on the list of symptoms that characterised Post Narcissist Stress Disorder, there was no longer an issue to write a second referral that included my upbringing in a narcissistic home.

So, now everything was fine, and I should be able to receive help. So we thought.

But the psychiatry clinic's answer was as follows: *There is no such thing as Post Narcissist Stress Disorder on our list of diagnoses and treatments.*

This way, people do not only keep a distance from individuals with personality disorders. They also maintain distance from those who are victims.

Here You Are, Some Information About PNSD From Power of Positivity [20]:

Much like Post Traumatic Stress Disorder, PNSD is a disorder that comes about after one has been living in close proximity to a narcissist. Living with a narcissist can be extremely taxing on a person. Narcissistic people tend to be extremely manipulative and abusive. They will often gaslight their victims and make everything about their own feelings.

After getting free of a narcissistic person's influence, people often experience a phase of helplessness, anxiety, anger, or depression, much like what happens after a traumatic event. People with PNSD react much like people who have PTSD. There are three major signs for someone who is suffering from Post Narcissist Stress Disorder.

- **Flashbacks**

Much like PTSD, PNSD can also cause the survivor of the narcissistic experience to have flashbacks of their time with the narcissistic individual. This can happen for any

---

[20]https://www.powerofpositivity.com/signs-post-narcissist-stress-disorder-pnsd/

reason. There are things called *triggers*. These can be any rage of things that cause a person to get *flashbacks* of their time with the narcissist.

According to the Royal College of Psychiatrists Public Education Committee, *"You find yourself re-living the event, again and again. This can happen both as a flashback in the day and as nightmares when you are asleep. These can be so realistic that it feels as though you are living through the experience all over again."* Triggers can be certain smells, some places, certain behaviour, or even some specific sounds or words.

Many people who suffer from PNSD may have a hard time dealing with other people's emotions because a narcissistic person will often fly into rage at the drop of a hat. That gives them jitters while dealing with other people.

Someone suffering from PNSD may be triggered into a flashback when they perceive someone as being upset or angry with them. The survivor may also get flashbacks to periods of manipulation from the narcissist. This may lead to extreme paranoia, where they wonder if the people around them are manipulating them. It may feel like they're playing a game they just can't win, even if no one around them has an ulterior motive.

- **Avoidance**

Someone who is suffering from PNSD may become avoidant of a number of things. This can manifest in avoidance of people, places, things, activities, or even emotions. Narcissistic individuals tend to control their victims, using manipulation and anger to keep them under their control. Even once the survivor is free from the narcissist's power, they may still exhibit PNSD in the form of avoidance.

Oftentimes, the survivors will avoid things that remind them of the narcissist's anger or things they weren't allowed to do while under the narcissist's influence. They may also become emotionally avoidant. People who are victims of narcissists will often be gaslighted into believing that their emotions are damaging to the narcissist. This may lead to someone with PNSD being distant from their emotions because they had to learn not to feel anything to survive the narcissist.

- **Difficulty Returning to a Normal Life**

One of the major symptoms of both PTSD and PNSD is extreme difficulty returning to normal life. For a person who is trying to return to a normal life after living with a narcissistic person, this may include anything from paranoia to panic attacks and even depression. Living with a narcissist can be extremely overwhelming, and someone who does so has to shift their expectations of day-to-day life.

They often have to learn to adapt to a 'new normal.' Afterwards, when they're removed from the narcissistic influence, the survivor may find it difficult to adjust to life again. They may have panic attacks, or they question their own memories and observations.

…

Remember what I wrote earlier. The psychiatry clinic's answer was as follows: *There is no such thing as Post Narcissist Stress Disorder on our list of treatments.*

This seriously was a diagnosis they didn't know about. Or didn't want to hear about it. I don't know. My curator shouldn't even use the words of PNSD, they told her. It may be a bit confusing, but one single traumatic event ends up with the quite same symptoms as long term experiences with a narcissistic family member. Trauma is not only about people being involved in car accidents or survivors of war. It's also about all of us who suffered through many years with a disordered person by our side.

Of course, these symptoms most likely also apply to the survivors of a psychopathic person. Worries stay within you despite the fact that the immediate danger is over. You may end up being worried and nervous about everything.

Beware of Men and Women Who...

The moral of this passage can possibly be discussed, and I know that I speak against my own existence when I say: Perhaps it's for the best if people with personality disorders never have children. Although my life today is extremely worth living, I wouldn't have been hurt from never being born. What you don't know can never hurt you... However, I have been hurt for many years of my life, and I know that not all children are able to break so strongly with their origin as I did. Dad, and many more, suffer all their lives.

A strong warning signal to check for when meeting a possible future life partner is that he or she agrees with you on *everything* you say. Whatever you say, there is a puppet nodding his or her head across the table. A person repeating a number of romantic phrases in a completely new relationship can in itself be a sign of nervousness, but it can also be a way to convince you that he or she is a real chap. Also, remember that what he or she tells you about oneself is not necessarily the reality. The behaviour is a better thing to go on. It is said that psychopathic people as love partners are difficult to interpret, that they are difficult to read. One moment they are soft and caring, and in the other, they come across as the opposite. Many women have testified a gross sexual behaviour in men. They may be obsessed with pornography, sometimes a violent kind, be extremely voluptuous and have sex without love as if the partner did not exist. Some of these women have said that the rough sexual behaviour has also affected their children.

In an interview in Näslund (2004), "Anna" says: *"Gather information and do some research on his background. How are his other relations in life? How did he grow up? If I had met his parents at the beginning of the relationship, I probably would have got suspicious pretty soon. A woman might be interested in starting an exciting relationship but then do not have children. Push the brakes when it comes to starting a family. Wait a few years and see how it turns out. This kind of men you shouldn't marry; they will not be good fathers."*

Further, "Anna," tells us about her psychopathic husband raping their daughter. A devastating fact that is not totally unusual for psychopathic men. And don't forget, there are mothers who 'sell' their daughters over the internet.

So, be together for a while before you have children. Go through a number of quarrels to see how your partner (without you calculating provokes him/her, of course, because then it is you who are mean) handles conflicts on occasions when his or her personality is put to the test. Don't judge too fast, neither be naïve. For example, when the person repeatedly says really mean things to you, but a second later smooths it over by saying 'it was a joke,' that is not healthy behaviour. This will tear you apart – just turn your back and leave. Through manipulation and psychological torture, you will eventually break down.

I know a woman who fell asleep totally exhausted every evening. Can you guess why? She was afraid she would be suffocated with a pillow after falling asleep. This couple is not together any longer. I also know a man who found a knife under his partner's mattress. They are not together any more either. It does not always end well:

"Emma was strong, determined and cheerful, but her family didn't recognise her since she met a new boyfriend. She became quiet and evasive, and she was very afraid of him. Finally, a relative reported to the police against her

will. Two weeks later, she was killed with exercise equipment as a weapon." [21]

We usually say that love is blind. At the beginning of a relationship, when love is really blind, is probably the period when the personality disordered partner throws his or her net. Be in love, but try to not go blind. Try to keep your mind clear. When your inner voice tells you things and gives red alerts, retreat as soon as you can.

Co-Dependency

I am a person who are used to adapt, and I still adapt to people too much sometimes. From time to time, I can feel the same energy my dad spread - the superior energy, which makes me agree to things I don't really want.

Nowadays, when things don't feel completely fine in a social situation, the bells often ring in my ears. It's warning bells telling me to stay put and keep as neutral as I can. It's important to know that being a former victim means that you are at risk to normalise bad situations. These situations might be so familiar to you that you simply don't react until it is too late in one way or another.

---

[21]https://utforskasinnet.se/5-tecken-pa-att-du-uppfostrar-narcissistiska-barn/

Something that might complicate situations even more, is that we do understand that a victim and the perpetrator is the same person. We may get caught up in a situation where we convince ourselves we must help and support the perpetrator. This is because we know that the perpetrator earlier in life was a victim, and we feel sorry for him or her. Unfortunately, this is something that a personality disordered person can take great advantage of. We need to remember that we don't want a world where people don't have to take responsibility for their own actions because, in the long run, that won't help anyone.

Further, it is important to know about the concept of co-dependency. Your tolerance is likely to increase concerning the psychopathic or narcissistic person's behaviour over time. To avoid further and even worse problems, you stay with him or her. You adapt. Acceptance is increasing, and it is a psychopathic or narcissistic person's big arena to manipulate you into this. Make you feel guilty. Every day you get worse poisoned; you feel it in your whole body and soul if you just take a second to reflect on your situation. Unfortunately, it is likely that you close your eyes and ears to the facts. The truth probably is that you cannot dare to leave. An intense fear makes you stand by the perpetrator and even defend him or her if acquaintances say something disadvantageous. You may also have accepted the fact that everything is your fault, that it is you who are "wrong," and that you don't deserve a better life, a better man or a better woman.

I have tried to talk to people in this particular state, I have begged them to try seeing through, but I have not reached them. Instead, what happens is that they react with irritation, frustration or anger over me "attacking" the person they are protecting. To get out of a relationship like this is terribly difficult and frightening, of course. Probably they don't have the strength to do anything about it. Though, sooner or later, they collapse completely. When I then ask them why they haven't heard my warnings and thoughts earlier, I get the answer *"I have been brainwashed"* and also the given answer *"I thought that the problems lay within me, that I was 'wrong'."*

It is a tough awakening realising thirty or forty years of life have passed with losing one's life for living through a disordered partner. When one has had the same thoughts as their partner, the same beliefs as them, and always chosen the same dish at the restaurant, it is devastating - realising that one stopped existing a long time ago. Probably it feels like life just disappeared. And probably it was the only life there was to live.

In a family with a disordered family member, there is a risk that the bonds which are usually created in a family through closeness, trust and love, are not created. When the children are grown up, family members lose touch with each other because there are no ties. However, it is even worse when the lack of love in the family leads to the continued narcissistic or psychopathic tendencies among future generations, as a result of children growing up to be like their parents. The negative legacy – the personality disorder, is adopted by future generations. This involves everything from fraudulent behaviour to death threats within the family.

When Two Narcissists Meet

When two narcissistic individuals meet as partners, companions or as friends, it does not necessarily mean that these two become enemies, as you might think. Instead, they may help each other to shine and raise each other to the skies. They do not share the same stage; instead, they emphasise each other. *"If you scratch my back, I will scratch yours."* [22]

It is a weird experience to watch two people, who you know can both be very mean in their narcissistic defences, fawn for each other – get so very cute and smooth. However, if they spend a lot of time together and over a period of time, they will get tired of stage-working for someone else. They don't want to share the attention. Investing in themselves is what they can handle in the long run. If they have committed to each other in economic or legal interests, it can turn into a battle of life and death. Both of them step up their narcissistic defences against each other. This can possibly be compared to having two roosters in one and the same hen house. They fight until one of them simply can no longer bear. Also, think for a second how this would turn out, or actually turns out, because it does happen, if these two are a couple with children.

---

[22]https://giftigarelationer.com/2017/11/29/skillnad-pa-narcissist-och-psykopat-vad-finns-dar-bakom/

The Narcissistic Mother

I know a woman who approached her thirties without wanting children. Nothing strange with that. But the reason that she didn't want to ruin her beautiful body seemed astounding. A short period later, we lost contact, and I don't know if she had any. Some people have children very late in life and only because they are aware of the fact that the biological clock is ticking. They feel that they must; otherwise, there won't be any. In that case, they may have children because it is something they should have to make their own lives perfect, not because they really want them. It would be best if you had children for the finest purpose and with the strongest will so that you could give the child a good life. The woman I mentioned appears in my memory when I read the following from Sandy Hotchkiss book *Why is it always about you?*

"Signs of a mother's narcissism are evident before the child is born in women who may be excessively preoccupied with their own appearance and comfort during pregnancy, who expects others to cater to them, who are unusually distressed with the changes in their bodies, or who are extremely fearful of labour and delivery. Some may be obsessed with having the perfect pregnancy or becoming a perfect mother. In other cases, a narcissistic mother-to-be may be too absorbed in her own life to seek adequate prenatal care or may engage in practices or activities, such as drugs or alcohol use or other risky behaviour, that endanger the fetus. She may show little interest in preparing for the arrival of the child, or conversely, she may be obsessed with having 'the best of everything', regardless of her financial circumstances. She may have excessive expectations in regard to gifts from relatives and friends or be more interested in decorating the nursery or assembling the layette than in actually welcoming a child into her life. The narcissistic mother to be maybe either detached from or overly invested in aspects of her pregnancy, but in either case, she is preoccupied with her own experience rather than focusing on the infant who will soon emerge from her body."

The continuation for this child is not expected to be positive. The mother is obsessed with having a perfect child, which she doesn't need to be ashamed of. She is trying to create another and more beautiful picture of the child. The actual child isn't worth as much as her "fantasy child," Her shortcomings as caretaker (when nobody is looking) will lead to abuse of the child, as everything shall suit her and her own needs. If she gets disappointed with her child, her shame and anger are triggered, which will affect the child in a devastating way.

This may trigger narcissism within the child, as the mother is unlikely to meet his or her needs. If her child makes a mistake, she will not reconcile with her child. Her own mistakes and failures will also affect the child, as she herself is not to blame. The shame will be imprinted in the child's body. Most likely, the child will not grow up to be a prosperous grown-up. There is a risk that the mother's narcissistic personality disorder passes over to the next generation.

Unfortunately, I have witnessed this behaviour in mothers. I clearly remember one example when a mother became very angry with her child because he couldn't walk obediently next to his mother for ninety minutes in a shop full of things that only the mother herself was interested in, and also without being allowed to touch anything. After one hour, the child got "noisy," at least the mother thought so. A heated exchange of words ensued, after which it was decided that the child would act according to his mother's needs instead of the other way round. Shopping done, the child was now punished. After ninety minutes in this store - a very long time for a three-year-old - no food was offered to the child.

He got an apple for dinner this late afternoon. This child also got yelled at for catching a cold because it stopped his mother's plans for the week.

Like my father and many other children in his generation, children of today also carry a lot of weight on their shoulders. They may take on the blame for things they can't help or influence - the often underlying phenomenon which, in time may lead to narcissism within a person. Maybe there are even more children who are experiencing this today? The thought frightens me.

Maybe you need to draw attention to someone close to you? Maybe you need to review yourself? Ask for help before someone else has to do it for you? A child cannot be expected to understand that something is wrong. Instead, he or she becomes deeply unhappy and starts believing that he/she is a wicked person who repeatedly does wrong, wrong, wrong... This will be hidden in the innermost corners of the heart until one day when it comes out all the more vehemently. This will be in another time, in another place, against another person...

The Good Parent and the Bad Parent

Narcissism may also be trigged within a child if a narcissistic or psychopathic parent is ravaging at home and does all sorts of harm to the children and the other parent, who, of course, takes on the role as a tremendous caretaker in an attempt to compensate. He or she then does *everything* for the children to comfort them and make them feel better. *They should not feel sad, they instead should get everything there can possibly be given.*

The children grow, and unfortunately, they may learn to exploit their parent's feelings for them. The children have been given the impression that he or she sets no limits, and it's sad to say, but as the parent is ageing, they start to exploit both financial possibilities and services. They may yell at the parent if services are not performed as earlier. The parent(s) may become afraid of their own children. Some narcissistic grown-up children may take advantage of their old parents until they can no longer cope, even until death.

Shared Custody

Shared custody with a personality disordered parent can be very difficult. During the stay in a narcissistic home, the children are not allowed to have their own thoughts and feelings. The parent puts himself in the first room at the expense of the children. The "love and care" from such parent is conditional, and the condition is becoming the way their parent wants them to be. This is happening at great expense of the children. The children who left home a week earlier are hardly the same when they come back.

Parents in this situation have experienced children coming home filled with unprocessed emotions felt through the emotional outbursts that follow the first days at home. There is anxiety in the air, and the least resistance may provoke an emotional outburst as if the evil that the children have been exposed to needs to pour out. It comes out in anger, crying and despair [23].

Parents with a personality disorder should not be caretakers in the first place. As you will read in this book, the disorders are often difficult to reveal. Both children and ex-partners do not trust anyone to believe them when they open up. Until this gets better, it is important that children are allowed to release the feelings they've been forced to

---

[23]https://giftigarelationer.com/2018/03/18/delad-vardnad-med-en-narcissist-det-ar-sallan-samma-barn-som-du-lamnade-som-kommer-hem/

keep inside when being abused or ignored in the past week. I hope that the healthy parent can cope emotionally and understand the child. It is crucial for the child to have one functional parental relationship. A parent in this situation needs to acquire knowledge about how to handle these difficult issues as long as shared custody is a fact. We should never forget to ask the children how we can help; their voices must be heard. Also, remember the fact that it is healthy for the child to react. I know that children sometimes keep their feelings inside until they break down in one way or another. It's dangerous. Outbursts are much safer because then we will notice something is wrong and get a chance to do something about the underlying problem.

Tricky Situation

It is not always easy to put your finger on problems in children's lives. It is not always noticeable. I had problems at school when I was a child; my classmates would bully me. This is sometimes the case with children from narcissistic or psychopathic families. They are used to not being anyone, so how can they be someone in school? Some children show disobedience to adults. I, however, allowed myself to disappear. Others do not succeed in their schoolwork because they don't have the strength. I studied until I felt sick because I learned from my home that resting isn't okay.

It is clear that it sometimes is difficult to discover children coming from unfavourable homes. However, this book will further show you some of the most incredible facts on this topic.

The Law

We talk a lot about children's rights, *The Convention on the Rights of the Child* is a familiar name to most of us. However, when problems approach in reality, we often don't stand up for these rights.

We find out about it from the newspapers. Despite people around the child having noticed warning signals earlier, 'a child has been abused to death in the home.' The news spreads, maybe a couple of days in a row, and then we go on with our lives as if nothing happened. We forget about it - every time.

On the morning of 10th of July 2011, a seven-year-old boy was murdered. The boy was stabbed seventeen times, and his life could not be saved. A man, 53 years old, was arrested for murdering the boy. The man was the boy's father, who admitted stabbing his boy but also claimed that he didn't mean to kill him.

The boy was at home with his father and his grandmother. The mother left for work earlier that morning. The grandmother was tricked into going outside, and she got locked out before the stabbing began. The grandmother tried to get help from the neighbours. Note that *the boy's mother had on several occasions reported the 53-year-old man for assault and threats.*

There are many people who are struggling to ensure that these children are not forgotten. I want to be a part of this; I want to remind everyone about them; they must stay in our memories. Many, along with me, are also struggling to change the future. Blunted as we are today, we now need to stop. To wake up, we need to try to see these events from the eyes of the child. To wake up, we need to force ourselves to see the dad coming towards us with a knife in his hand. We need to imagine this boy's fear and pain when the knife hit him seventeen times. If we close our eyes to this reality, while sitting in the 21st-century jet plane, it will pass us as well – and the world will be the same tomorrow...

Sometimes in our society, parents' rights to the child seem to be more important than children's rights to a safe and happy life. In some countries, it doesn't even matter if a parent has been locked up in prison for abusing his child, and his ex-partner describes him as psychopathic according to the checklists. It doesn't matter if we can read the child and notice that something is wrong. If that doesn't matter, what can we do? The child is forced to stay in the parents care anyway.

Sometimes it doesn't even matter if the children have seen their mother getting murdered by their father. The father gets to keep custody from inside the prison. From the cell, he has the power to control the children. For example, he can refuse psychological help on their behalf, and the children are forced to cooperate with him. That is something we can't believe is possible in a civilised society, but it has been reported on several occasions even there.

Would you like to have a caregiver whom you've seen murdered a dear one? Murder at all? Even hit someone? There must be a stop to this. There must be a point where no arguments can break through. Don't you agree?

There also have been children begging not to go home for fear of receiving a beating and are sent home anyway to get killed. When children like this later are found dead, the autopsy shows that the bodies have been abused for several months. It gets even more frustrating when you find out that misery has actually been revealed in these families in earlier instances as well. This should not be possible. It's more than heartbreaking. There are no words to explain that.

Healthcare professionals usually have an insight into people's homes that other groups rarely have. When they are in someone's home, it happens that they get to see home conditions in which children shouldn't stay. They report their concerns in line with their obligations, but they cannot count on any changes when they at the next occasion arrive with the ambulance visiting the home where a child has "injured himself" in an impossible way. Again. It is clear that we lack the capacity to make a difference when it comes to safety for children.

Who Will Save the Children?

According to me, there are five ways in which narcissism and psychopathy (and other disorders and problems for that matter) can be revealed in a family:

- The personality disordered parent discovers that something is wrong and acts by seeking help. (It happens that narcissistic individuals seek help when they have noticed that, for example, their career or relationship is negatively affected by the disorder, even if it is rare. Psychopathic individuals do not usually seek help for their condition).

- The other adult in the family – the partner – receives information and knowledge and realises what the family is actually affected by, and then take necessary action.

- Someone from outside the family, a relative, social authorities, police, nursing staff or school get a view of patterns and act.

- The law, as a result of the previous points, steps in to protect children.

- If none of these "protective barriers" work, then only the children can save themselves. It is far from all children who succeed.

Children Are Not Seen

We can't count on the personality disordered parent himself to do something to solve the problem. Commonly, what happens is that the healthy parent reacts and acts, but you will soon know how that often turns out. In some countries, we can also discover that the routines of legal forces, public healthcare, social services and school haven't served well enough as protective factors for children. In a report, we can read:

- Family psychiatry healthcare is good for the parents but not for children

- Family psychiatry healthcare is family-oriented, not focused on the child.

- Lack of resources in school

- School doesn't see the signals

- Social services haven't seen and understood [24]

Parents I have been talking to have experienced extreme rejection when seeking help from authorities, thereby their children find themselves in a situation without protection. Sometimes parents have received the most inconceivable arguments from the authorities, as they try to avoid unpleasant subjects and make the parents and applicants insecure, stopping them from moving on with their case. They also have experienced authorities temporising their point of view to suit the persons they are addressing.

---

[24] Engström, L & F (2012) *Vad får maskrosorna att växa?* Umeå universitet.

In situations with narcissistic and psychopathic individuals manipulating, provoking or threatening them, people on the mission to protect children sometimes get scared or uncertain about future prospects. These disordered personalities can push others immensely, sometimes with pure lies, to the point that not even well-educated authority-staff can see situations clearly, dare to act or have the strength to resist persuasion. I hope that the awareness and knowledge concerning this huge problem will increase and that parents of the affected children get the required help and trust from others. The parents are trying to save their children. You can't tell a parent in this situation to take their words back and get silent on the matter.

The bullet list regarding family, psychiatry, healthcare, school and social services above comes from a study of Dandelion Children (children who are able to create a functional life as adults, despite a less favourable upbringing) carried out at a Swedish university. In this study, Dandelion Children reveal their experiences concerning the absence of help they should have received as children. Parents' experiences of lacking support and protection in the modern world are confirmed by Dandelion Children who are adults today. This means the problem has been going on for several decades. The affected grown-up children expressed that no one saw their vulnerability when they were young. They emphasise the importance of having interested adults. By reading the study, I understand that they mean *genuinely interested*. That underscores the shortcomings of society in protecting these children.

When the Dandelion Children tell us that adults didn't see the signals, I wonder if they really didn't see or understand or if they simply didn't dare to listen. These are painful questions.

Social services and other authorities have meetings with affected children. The experiences from these meetings are sometimes negative. Several parents share their experiences and highlight the following concern: The authorities listen to the children if they say something that fits them; something that makes the cases easier to handle. If they say something that makes the matter difficult or unpleasant, adults are told not to listen so much to the children.

Their children are persuaded to continue living with parents who hurt them in one way or another. *"...But it's your dad/mum..." "...But dad/mum also wants to spend time with you..."* There may even have been a verdict over the other parent, a verdict that shows that something is wrong.

There may have come signals from school, but still, the child is persuaded to bear with their inadequate parent. The parent's rights and access to the child seem to be more important than the well-being of the child. Eventually, the child falls into silence.

If the child doesn't fall silent and instead continues to cry over the fact that he or she is going to the disordered parent, there is a risk that the healthy parent is accused of causing tears in the child's eyes and putting the words into the child's mouth.

Now, stop here for a short while, and try to feel how you almost get suffocated by your own feelings from being dependent on adults who hurt you. You are not able to do something about your situation because the adults are in power. They may be mean to you every day, but no one sees it or believes in you as a child. Once or twice you may have tried to put your foot down only to get beaten for what you did. You may also have met a few people seeing in whose eyes you could tell they understood your situation and believed in you, but in the same eyes, you could spot fear too. In the following interactions, this person may say things to downplay your observations and experiences because he or she doesn't want inconveniences. It's easier for them to just walk away. You are then left with no option other than to go back to your home. You cannot pack your belongings and leave "your home." You need food and clothing to survive. If you try to escape, you will be found, and then you don't know what will happen when you come home next.

Many children don't even understand that something can be wrong in their families. I'm one of them. The children who do understand and open their hearts must be listened to. Probably they are afraid of the consequences if they "gossip," but then you can also imagine how much these children suffer when they ultimately find revealing the truth the only way out.

All of us who are working in school have probably met children that don't seem to feel very well inside. We get a feeling, and we ask. They say nothing. They show nothing. That leaves us feeling unsatisfied on our part. But if we don't want them to speak either, for fear of inconveniences, what else can they do then? When are adults satisfied?

A thought that sometimes sweeps through my mind is that the position of authority that adults assume in children's lives might sometimes lead us to avoid problems. That way, we will end up protecting the adults instead of children. We have the power to choose and make decisions on how to act when we receive information. If we choose not to act, the result will be adults protecting one other. We put the parent's satisfaction on the top priority, along with peace in our own lives. This is often at the great expense of children's welfare - the children who are in a position of dependence. Maintaining the friendship with the parents or other adults, for that matter, must never be more important than acting in the children's best interest.

When it comes to professionals, it is important to show each other respect for our respective competence. Of course, professionals and authorities have to be objective and impartial in their judgements; there are no two ways about that. That is important and it concerns school, social services, family psychiatry, healthcare, police and other important departments. However, with increased knowledge regarding people with personality disorders, whose "main-competence" may be manipulation, we can reduce suffering. A person with a personality disorder can, without human knowledge and awareness, seem slippery like an eel. If you learn to see patterns, the eel may not be so slippery any longer. The lies and manipulations may appear quite obvious and therefore possible to see through. For example, *why has the person changed his or her mind since last the last occasion?* Why not ask some questions about it? Knowing that a narcissistic or a psychopathic individual is chasing benefits, we can learn to see through them.

There are children who have been forced to stay in destructive environments as a consequence of adults not caring to see or being blind to what's hiding in the dark. I am convinced, however, that it is possible to learn to see through these people by being well-read, good listeners and by taking lessons from second-hand experiences. By taking part in people's experiences, we gain experience ourselves. I am well aware of the fact that it is difficult to reach victims and break negative patterns in families. Lots of people work with it daily, and they may not always succeed. An enormous number of people choose their career with the motivation: *"...because then I can help people."* It isn't that friendly men and women are missing in our society. But it seems that we have to learn new things, find new paths, courage and strength. My own experience tells me that people get very confused and scared when unpleasant information comes out. The fact that a parent may suffer from a personality disorder is such an area. We simply become unsure if it really is reasonable to believe so, we do not want to blame anyone, and we really don't want to get involved in an unpleasant fight. Therefore, there is an overwhelming risk that we keep too much distance in the matter. No doubt, narcissism and psychopathy are simply issues that people want to avoid talking about. These disorders evoke strong emotions.

"Complicated" is a term often used to cover the underlying narcissistic and psychopathic tendencies. *"It's a complicated matter."* In this context, there is a risk of us keeping too much distance or maybe wrapping the information up before moving on to the next instance. In our mind, we say to ourselves: *We might be wrong... with a little caution, the information will not be so accusing and sharp against anybody.* Now, the risk is, of course, that the information at this time is so wrapped up and diffused that it is often missed. I have studied literature in the field and understood that it is not only the fear of acting that makes these cases difficult to handle in a stable and clear manner, but sufficient knowledge is also lacking in this regard. Authorities such as schools and social services need more education to be able to succeed in their work. The people who have the intention to play a positive role and who from the beginning focused their career on helping people also need support from the legalisation in order to carry out their heroic efforts.

To me, it seems hopeless if fear, ignorance and regulations cause obstacles. Who will save the children from growing up wing-broken or as a new generation of narcissistic and psychopathic individuals? They get poisoned. Society as a protective barrier seems to fall apart in these matters. Keep in mind that you don't have to scream with your loudest voice immediately when you suspect children getting hurt from these disorders in a non-life-threatening kind of way; you can start by paying attention to children's behaviour and finding out how to best nurture them while you try to find out more about it. You can also carefully listen to the parent who has valuable information to give. And of course, to the children even if it gets unpleasant.

Further, the children need to be allowed to take part in decisions concerning their future. Where do they need to live to have a chance of saving their future? Hence, the children must then not be affected by pressures such as threats or manipulation while giving their views on the matter. The risk is great, so try to see through it. If a personality disordered parent exercises influence by being able to contact the child at any time, well, we can only guess what would happen next. The child would have no option other than acting diplomatically. When the child or the other parent agrees to claims in the matter of contact, the risk is imminent that the personality disordered parent devours the whole child by hauling in, threatening and manipulating.

How many of us suffer from psychopathy or psychopathic features is unclear because different researchers come to varied conclusions. I have therefore chosen to present the result anywhere between one to three per cent. Some say more; others say less. Is it then so unlikely that authorities such as social services and schools actually meet psychopathic parents? In a school with four hundred students, we may have, on average, four to twelve parents with psychopathic traits with probably at least eight affected children. And then they become adults, maybe with the same traits, or broken in other ways... As far as narcissism is concerned, the number usually figure between two and four per cent of all adults, but there is a hint that narcissistic personality disorder is even more common. And then their children grow up too...

Men *and* Women

I know several families who have had contact with authorities because of major problems in the family, of exactly the kind we are discussing in this book. In these cases, it is often mothers that have revealed the problems, but it can also be fathers, of course. I once encountered and knew a woman whom I, after a rather long period of time, realised was suffering from psychopathic traits, to put it mildly. When I had subsequently thought through her reasoning and her plan to get custody of the children, I realised that the father probably was finding himself in the same situation as the mothers in following pieces. It didn't sound at all like the plan was about the children or their best interest. It was about her and her alone.

It can also be mentioned that studies and statistics suggest that most narcissistic and psychopathic individuals are men. But despite the fact that most psychopathic people in *prison* are men, we should not take for granted that there are not so many women who suffer from these disorders. Men possibly end up in jail more often because of a more masculine and violent kind of psychopathy and therefore are counted in statistics to a greater extent. However, women certainly cause great mental damage and then slip away before they're revealed. Women more often use passive aggression, a breakdown of other people over time. There may be a great estimated number of unknown cases regarding the women. The psychopathic mother may, like a father, appear very devoted, caring and loving, while she treats her children as her property. She doesn't refrain from using them – or getting rid of them – for satisfying her own selfish needs. However, it is suggested in the current situation that there are three times as many psychopathic men than women [25].

Following is some information I have collected about mothers I 've met, who have been exposed by fathers.

Who Is to Believe?

In the family, there has been both physical and mental abuse for a long time. It started even before the children were born, but with the influence of oppression, the woman didn't believe that she was worth more. She was lucky to have a man at all!

---

[25] Kreis, M, Hoff. H.A, Belfrage, H & Hart, S (2016) *Psykopati.* Studentlitteratur.

After a long process in the land of awakening, the mother explains the situation and tries to get help. She is at this time very weak after a long period of abuse, and she needs ALL help that she possible can receive.

But then the "fantastic and devoted" father appears in the context, and suddenly, there cannot exist any problems anymore. *What a wonderful dad! A family with such a nice father can't possibly have problems!*

Turn it around:

- Why is the concept of difficulties and problems with such a perfect man in the family even mentioned?

- Why does the mother experience fear when she is married to such a divine man?

- Why does the family feel so bad?

It is a well-known fact that it is positive to form your own opinion of people. We should not listen to wicked rumours that may lead people to social exclusion. It is really important to develop our own opinion. When personality disordered people are in our vicinity, however, nothing works the way it normally does. You may have been strongly warned, but hear yourself say, *"But... he was a nice guy!"* or *"There was nothing wrong with her! A very nice person!"*

In a case where a parent comes and tells you about a behaviour, it is important for you to have knowledge about how a person with a personality disorder behaves to get a fair idea of the real situation. Without knowledge, it is impossible to discover the problems. The worst scenario, the most devastating, the most painful experience a mother in this situation can be exposed to is as follows *"It may be the mother who is lying, who exaggerates the whole story."*

Then imagine that you are the mother who has just realised that there is nothing wrong with *you*; it's not you who are the crazy one, something you have been tricked into believing for so many years. I refer to previous chapters in this book and a lot of alternative literature. For a long period of time, your manipulative husband may have made you believe that you are a completely useless person in all areas, and yes, maybe even crazy. You have been manipulated, deceived, threatened and abused, along with your children. Against all odds, you find the strength to confront that your husband has made you believe that you are completely crazy and useless for a long time. Once you are sitting there, and you need help like never before, they don't believe you. You are not taken seriously. And if the authorities, in fact, really suspect that you are a little crazy and that your purpose is to defame your gentlemanly husband… How would you feel?

Eva Rusz is an author who empowers women and also men in her books on this subject. She writes about a number of men who work as pilots, teachers, doctors and psychologists and perform their duties exemplary, but also commit criminal acts at home against their family, such as threatening and abusing them. Note the fact that we are talking about men with a significant socio-economic status… One of the examples is Martin Trenneborg, who passed a five-year medical education without a single negative remark in his academic career and held the reputation of being a caring physician with no problems taking on responsibilities. A popular doctor. At home, however, he held a woman locked up in a bunker on his farm. People generally hold such professionals in high regard. They, for example, believe that a doctor, without any doubt, is a friendly person, that a pre-school teacher is kind, etc. Unfortunately, I once met a pre-school teacher who had adopted four children. The story of their upbringing arrived ten years later, and a very upsetting story it was. Nobody could think that something would be wrong; she was a "pre-school teacher mum."

Another example that Eva Rusz mentions is American Ted Bundy, who was also a very competent student. At first, he studied to be a psychologist, and then he studied to be a lawyer. But he murdered thirty women, the youngest twelve years old, by crushing their heads. He raped them both before and after death. (Imagine that one of these women was your daughter, sister, mother or wife). A female professor in psychology stated that it *"is completely impossible for Ted to be a killer and she would do everything in her power to support him regarding the mean accusations levelled against him."* Some time passed, and it became clear – he was the killer.

Eva Rusz levels sharp criticism against Robert Hare's checklist of Psychopathy symptoms. The second example, Ted Bundy, had zero in all criteria because of his education, he was engaged in politics, and he supported suicidal students. These are the people who outwardly are so incredibly well-behaved, so much so that when partners tell their true story, nobody believes them. They may have been persecuted, manipulated, harassed, abused, threatened but are not believed. The psychopathic individuals get away with all the charges, as in the courtroom, they show a personality that makes it impossible for others to believe that they have done something wrong. According to Eva Rusz, a woman (or a man) who has lived with a psychopathic person for a long time and reports to the police can be exposed to counter-questions and statements which sound like these:

- And what did you do then? You are two parts in the relationship…

- We should be careful in making a diagnosis; only certain experts in psychiatry are allowed to do that / can do that.

- The diagnosis of psychopathy? No, that diagnosis is based on people with criminal behaviour, and they usually are in prison.

- Your partner is functional at his work, and in the social life, so you can forget about a diagnosis like that one!

- Your partner may be emotionally vulnerable, immature or he might suffer from another kind of diagnosis.

One woman says that she had met three experienced specialists in psychiatry, two licensed psychotherapists and a psychologist, who believed there was nothing wrong with her partner, despite the fact that he had cut her underwear into pieces when she didn't do as was told. She herself was told by these experts that she was emotionally vulnerable, that she exaggerated, and she also was asked, *"What did you do to contribute to this misunderstanding?"* Rusz further explains that the experts' advice in many cases has aggravated the situation. There is no chance they would put the diagnosis to revealing psychopathy, and they do not believe in people who are exposed to such evil. Sometimes the victim ends up being injured for life or murdered by her or his partner. The experts distance themselves from psychopathy because it is less dramatic to centre the diagnosis around ADHD, Asperger's syndrome, psychosis, depression, Tourette's syndrome, schizophrenia, post-traumatic stress disorder, narcissistic personality disorder or Borderline. Psychopathy is excluded. So either it's one of those diagnoses, or there is nothing wrong with him at all, as it may seem like that outwardly. Now, the fear of psychopathy leads to a risk of putting the wrong diagnosis, which further leads to incorrect treatment and then, of course, no proper attention to the children in the family is paid. And again, sometimes, the victims end up being injured for life or murdered. I agree with Rusz when she writes, *"If you have been through it, you know. Then you yourself are the expert."*

I must ask how anyone can believe that a planned meeting with a manipulative person and a professional present can compete with the experiences from many years of everyday life in a relationship. That is, of course, if you are interested in the dark truth and in how the person really works. But what can we do when a psychopathic person is capable of and maybe also allowed to manipulate the psychologists, the therapists, and the whole courtroom? Examine the person more closely despite his perfect appearance and his education and success? Provoke an outburst? Try to find evidence? Learn more about the treacherous of manipulative behaviours?

I know of a situation where a man agreed to go into therapy because he knew he was psychopathic. The problem was that he manipulated the therapist, so they didn't get anywhere with the treatment. There seem to be at least two explanations as to how psychopathic individuals can continue to ravage freely. First, their ability to manipulate and thereby their ability to get off the hook and second, the concept of psychopathy, or the loaded word "Psychopath," scares everyone off, including the professionals who should be able to see through and discover the dysfunctional patterns which lie behind the problems.

Imposters

On the news, they announce that "romance scams" have increased drastically over the years and that it is recidivists that are the villains. The concept of psychopathy, a word that the listeners should hear once in a while, is conspicuous as it is not clearly apparent. Of course, there are other several diagnoses that might be the explanation for the behaviour, such as narcissism and borderline, but my point here is that people are deceived all over again because they don't know about the warning signs. They don't know what it's about. They lack knowledge concerning how to protect themselves. Maybe psychopathy are still only about serial killers? We need to get rid of that image. People need to know that this is a common scenario when personality-disordered individuals are nearby. We must not think that we just were unlucky to meet a bad man or woman. We must get the chance to at least begin to understand, to be able to act long-term.

There is a woman on the news this day, telling her story:

"He seemed to be a very nice, normal and charming man. He seemed kind, and he was good-looking too (...). When I talk about this afterwards, it feels obvious that

something must have been wrong, but when he explained and talked about it, it sounded so genuine."

The news also reports that the police at the time received a lot of reports every day concerning romance frauds, and the man in question had cheated women of millions. That is exactly what often happens with a personality disordered person in the equation. They seem so fantastic or present themselves as people in need, as victims of unfortunate circumstances, and exploit the partner's finances. The money in the bank account is spent first, and then it continues with "saving the situation" with loans from different banks.

Only when payment is required, there are no possibilities left to lend more money, and the partner is gone; he or she understands what happened. Or not. Perhaps one just had bad luck meeting a bad person...

A Phone Call

A few years ago, I took part in a phone call between a father, who definitely suffered from a personality disorder, and his daughter. Her mother had been struggling for a long time with her, what it seemed, psychopathic ex-husband. The daughter now felt strong enough to tell her teachers at school how she and her siblings were treated by their dad at home. The girl had had enough, felt brave at the moment and in this conversation, she did not give in to her father. The conversation was a roller-coaster between being nice by manipulation, violations and threats on the father's behalf. When one way didn't work, he tried the other way, and when that didn't work either, he started again from the beginning. A desperate father who understood or did not understand that he had gone too far. Again.

What he exposed his daughter to in this conversation was, without any doubts, psychological torture. She is, though, one of those children who have a chance as an adult to become strong and independent and become different from her father. She may be able to break the social heritage and become one of the children who succeeds in saving herself, also called *a Dandelion child*.

Her family has, for a long time, been known by both social services and police. The father had been in prison for assaulting one of his children. He has also abused others in his family both physically and psychologically for many years. Still, he succeeded to get into the family over and over again by threatening family members. How is this possible?

Locked Position

Sometimes family issues get stuck in a locked position. The following are based on a couple of mother's experiences.

- Due to certain circumstances, the father has, in fact, now, after a long period of time, been declared unfit regarding custody. He has a schedule with only a few occasions a month, after which he can spend time with his children.

- Social services are connected; the mother opens up and shares information that earlier has been family secrets.

- She registers that she doesn't reach through to the social services with her information of what she has seen and experienced, the fear and powerlessness. She is told that she should encourage her children to spend time with the father.

- The father puts pressure under threats and by using manipulation. He uses the mother to get access to the children and the children to get access to the mother. This is because he wants more time with the children. It means financial contributions on his part to take care of them. Since the mother has custody, she is the one to decide, and he knows about it. Manipulating or threatening the mother and children is nothing that worries him.

- Eventually, the mother gives in to his request. She doesn't dare to deny him to spend more time with the children.

- If she applies for a new hearing in court to stop the father from spending time with the children or cause other changes, it will be seen as a completely new case.

- Then the mother is afraid of losing, aware of the highly manipulative and lying capacity within her ex-partner. The ex-partner can and will take the chance to present himself as a completely changed, and maybe even reborn human being. The mother fears that the court next time won't see through who he really is, which is likely to be devastating to the children. She is afraid to take on this risk.

One thought: If we look back at the fourth point, should we really put this on an already vulnerable parent to decide how much time he can spend with the children when she is begging on her knees for the authorities to take on the responsibility and say no to him in her place? He forces her to give in a little bit, and then he hauls them in completely.

Wouldn't it be safer for the children if someone else than the mother could step in and draw the line? He has been in prison for assaulting a child in a serious manner, for crying out loud!

A person with a personality disorder is in many cases "allowed" to continue threatening the children and the other parent. As long as he or she is allowed to fly under the radar and the healthy parent has to make these decisions, we are risking these locked positions. Some parents have experienced that the authorities are hiding behind their backs; *"We are not the ones to decide; you have to ask your ex-partner."* However, it is sometimes the children who, against their own will, are forced to convey over a phone call to the healthy and threatened parent, with the disordered sitting next to them. They do not dare to say *No*.

By authorities, these disputes sometimes are seen as conflicts between two equally functional caregivers, and it is therefore assumed that it is the conflict between the parents which serves to explain the children's anxiety. They assume that the parents' conflict causes conflicts within the children because the children want to satisfy them both. They call it a "conflict of loyalty."

If the children are strong enough to reveal the reasons as to why they don't want to live with the other parent, it still is steered towards the fact that it is the loyalty conflict that causes the problems. There are cases where authorities have told the children that *"dad/mum will become sad if he/she isn't allowed to be with you."* Of course, this means a great risk of adults provoking the "loyalty conflict" which they later themselves refer to. It is perceived by parents that there may be a risk for information concerning our children getting manipulated through the system. According to them, you sometimes reinforce the information you want to hear and weaken the information you don't want in the case. This will take the edge off the kind of information which is perhaps the most important.

After taking part in parents' stories, one may get the impression that authorities *want* it to be conflicts of loyalty. This way you don't have to choose a side. Authorities certainly strive with the fact that they must be impartial. We have to respect that, of course. However, this has also happened in situations where the children's problems regarding one of the parents are obvious.

Although there are professionally successful psychopathic individuals like Ted Bundy and Martin

Trenneborg, doctors, psychologists, and lawyers, there are also individuals who have failed financial success. This might be explained by the fact that they're not always functional in cooperating with other people. If they take care of their children, they may receive economic or social assistance. However, it is not at all certain that the money benefits the children. I know children who have been offered only a sandwich to eat for days during the stay and no trips whatsoever. When the children leave, the parent spends the money on him- /herself. In these cases, I think that it would be justified to demand a receipt. What was the money spent on? Did they visit the zoo? The cinema? Did they buy new jeans? It is important that the children don't end up in trouble; they should never be forced to lie. Maybe demanding receipts seems harsh, but sometimes you don't find the ultimate right. Instead, you have to seek the least wrong way to handle things and to reveal bad behaviour.

With what we now have read regarding personality disorders, things have to change. We cannot continue to allow children growing up wing broken, mentally or physically, perhaps also sexually abused. To gain knowledge about personality disorders is, of course, a vital element if we ever should be able to change this. We have to start listening to the victims and try our best to see through. We also must remember that there is no point in listening if we aren't prepared to act. A parent with a personality disorder should not be allowed to take care of children. Also, don't forget that manipulative traits exist. It's easily happened to be fooled. To be a part of this "game" can, of course, become devastating to a child's development. They need protection. These disorders have been confirmed for a very long period of time. Even if the children have a strong mother...

Therapist: *You should take my advice and file for divorce.*

Mother: *But I have children...*

Therapist: *That's exactly why* [26].

...who acts according to a therapist's advice and leaves her husband, there is still absolutely no guarantee that she will receive support in going ahead with the divorce and thereby protect the children. The children, who still will be left partly with their father, are at risk of being strongly influenced by his inappropriate way of being. They may take an influence from him or be crushed by him. The more

---

[26] Näslund G.K (2004) *Lär känna psykopaten.* Natur och kultur

threatened he perceives himself to be by his ex-partner and maybe also by the authorities, the more threatening he will become when nobody sees him in action. The mother then no longer has the insight and the power to protect her children. She is no longer around. The mother and the children now instead are exposed to domestic violence for trying to leave. When a victim leaves her partner, one is not going to be left alone. Sabotage, stalking, abuse, tormenting a pet or children being used as tools in a long and very contentious custody dispute are common in these situations. Parents suffering from personality disorder have an extremely powerful appearance in front of their children. They want blind obedience from their children. They will show that they are at the top of the world. The children are emotionally forced to give him what he needs and confirm to his terms. They know what is expected from them. The mother is threatened and at risk for her children being turned against her on her ex-partner's initiative. This will probably lead to him getting his way even more. The social services are manipulated, and the children are at risk of becoming a copy of their father, especially if they are still young children. Society, in fact, *we,* if we don't open our eyes, still see a well-dressed, nice and devoted father who loves his children.

If he is suffering from psychopathy, he probably has been studying how parents usually show emotions and empathy, and he will adeptly recreate and demonstrate these behaviours. He may claim to love his children, but a psychopathic person most likely doesn't know what genuine love means. He needs them to satisfy his own needs, and it is possible that he in his state perceives the feeling to be favoured as love.

There are disordered parents who give their children sleeping pills when they are tired of them. They may want some peace and quiet or go to a party instead of being babysitters. These parents simply lack the ability to be functional parents.

What I now have been writing about the lack of knowledge and lack of support from authorities is shared from different mothers, who don't know about each other. They are telling exactly the same story. These stories are their experiences. Do not forget that the perpetrator can also be a woman.

Another Parent's Story

"You should know that it has taken my children a very long time to dare to share the truth. Everything is going

wrong in their lives. They are ashamed of how they are treated, though they aren't the ones to be ashamed. They take on the blame even though the fault is not theirs. Them bringing it up takes a lot of courage. They have been exposed to an abusive and threatening adult for several years. This is a person who has shown a different personality outwards than when she has been alone with my children.

Is it logical to think they would lie when they are afraid to tell, and the person in question gets worse and worse in her defence? My experiences meeting the authorities regarding the difficult situation that my children have been exposed to is that separate institutions within the authorities are hiding behind each other's back. If it is already a family law matter, they choose not to act. This is so incredibly wrong. The legal process has taken a long time, and my children have now been in danger for several years before it is even heard in the court of law. Before the case arrives in court, the evidence is not paid attention to.

Until then, this woman has been able to lie and manipulate freely. In my children's lives, this has failed so many times along the way. Things that have happened and things that my children have been sharing should have been reported by everyone who has heard their stories. New things have happened all the time. But instead of reporting, it is written in red as examples in their health records. But then what? Why hasn't the school nurse reported to social services? The information does no good in a dusty folder on her shelf... The information could have been used for the process to speed up. Social services have tried to diminish our case by saying: "Well, nobody is dead, so the children's stories might not be so serious."

The only thing that remains to do is to protect and strengthen the children. Back them up in daring to speak out when they are harassed. But when adults living in destructive relations don't dare to stand up for themselves, how can we expect that children will be able to do so without support? As a parent, you find yourself powerless. I have been forced just to stand here, watching my children being destroyed by another person."

Now, a period of time has passed since this parent shared this information with me. Therefore, I know that this parent finally won the case in the court of law with the help of all her evidence. By that time, though, several years of abuse and suffering had passed, and symptoms within the children became quite visible.

Proof

One thing we need to amplify is the problems that may arise when these cases arrive in court. It is important to be aware of and gain knowledge regarding personality disorders, working with these family cases. Divorced *functional* parents, of course, don't end up in the court of law every day.

You also need to be brave. A scenario where you take one part after another out of context won't benefit the children. Victims have been told: *"All people are lying sometimes," "All people lose control sometimes," "All people lack empathy sometimes," "All people sometimes exploit others…"* You should add the puzzle of betrayal and destructiveness and use your knowledge together with this information to see through the situation.

From experience, I have understood that these problems are relatively common. This is because either those I have spoken to directly or someone close to them has been exposed. Most recently, I heard of a very well-behaved man, well-dressed, sweet-smelling and very pleasant, who spent his nights vandalising his ex-partner's home in the most twisted ways one can imagine. Those who work in the court and judge in cases like these must have seen patterns and similarities many times, at least the experienced ones. Still, victims get to hear the most incomprehensible excuses and statements one can imagine from lawyers and judges. These cases can, of course, become difficult because there are sitting manipulative individuals on the other side of the table. Maybe not even a judge with solid experience and solid knowledge, in the end, knows which leg to stand on, but with awareness, perhaps the right questions can be asked.

Parents also have experienced that the outcome of a trial may be due to who you meet in court. I'm wondering about factors and explanations for their statements. It doesn't seem so reliable that the outcome depends on who is working with the case and who you happen to meet in court. This can also take place in the one and same district court concerning one and the same family. Does it depend on the judge's private experiences? The judge's knowledge? Whether it is a man or a woman? How many years of experiences they have? How easily they can be manipulated? As I said, it doesn't seem very reliable.

The situation may also have grown bigger than within the family. School, social services, and other authorities may have supported the victims at first, but when it heats up, strong fear may arise. A manipulative man or woman may also have gained statements from staff working in a school, or social services, which then are used against them. Others start to lie instead, to protect themselves. The psychopathic person then can let go of the lying tendencies for a little while because there are others who are lying in his stead. Glances are going in new directions, and that can be turned into a game, a chessboard, where benefits are to be found. This way, many people around these cases may become victims without understanding the game. Documentation "disappears" because people want to protect themselves, information is withheld, people's stories change... What they said yesterday no longer applies, and people involved start blaming each other to protect themselves.

If the psychopathic person happens to know someone or is related to someone within the authorities, the case may become very complicated. This employee risks being accused of conflicts of interest as a direct consequence of the personality disordered's actions that have exploited their relation.

To You Experiencing a Custody Dispute with a Narcissistic or Psychopathic Person

There is advice to read in both books as well as online for those of you who are having a difficult time. Try to find the time and energy to read a little. Only realising the fact that you are not alone may strengthen you. If I were you and I didn't have children together with the person in question, I would immediately leave after realising his truth. A psychopathic person is easily offended, which may lead to anger. Be very careful how you present your position when you end the relationship. *"I feel / experience that I…"* instead of *"You are… It's your fault…"* Instead of blaming, it's better to mould your message towards the fact that it is about you and your life, and maybe your plans for the future. You may not want to be alone with him/her in the house when you present your version. Maybe you should visit a restaurant and avoid following him/her back home afterwards or just pack your bags and leave when he/she is at work. Go to parents and friends. This is a difficult decision, which only you can make.

Earlier, you have read that it may be very difficult to prove what you have been exposed to afterwards. Do you remember the well-behaved, well-dressed, sweet-smelling and very pleasant man who spent his nights vandalising his ex-partner's home? If you've got evidence in the form of recordings, witnesses writing down, pictures of your body after abuse… save them. And give these shreds of evidence to a dear friend or a relative; do not keep them in your home. Get support from family or friends. Do what you can to leave safely. If your partner is disordered, remember that you may be tapped or filmed in your own home. He or she may also sneak up on you.

If you have children – be happy about the fact that the children at least have *one* functional parent, you. There are children who don't have anyone fighting for them. When it comes to exposing a narcissistic or psychopathic partner, remember to put all possible evidence away in a safe place. A psychopathic person, if you are sure you're dealing with one, should not take care of children, at least not if he or she early in life didn't learn the difference between right and wrong. Even if this is the case, there always need to be an emotionally healthy person present in children's lives while growing up. A narcissistic person should not take care of children either. In case of such a person present in children's lives, he or she needs to receive successful therapy, admitting the problems back in time, and really work hard towards curing themselves.

Maybe you are afraid of revealing what's going on in the family. You are aware of the fact that things easily can be turned around so that others will believe that you are the lying or deceptive person. Many victims claim that they aren't trusted. A family counsellor may be able to help you. However, keep in mind that, in the long run, it is no alternative to staying with your partner.

Psychopathic traits often show up already in early childhood, and I agree with people who say that it is possible to do something about it. This book is partly about disordered people and their experiences as children. Some of them were exposed to psychopathic caregivers themselves when they grew up. I understand that those who claim that a solution to this problem doesn't exist refer to adults who suffer from the disorder. However, our attitude must be one of bringing a change in this issue; otherwise, we may just give it all up. If everyone gives up, it will lead to even more children growing up in the care of disordered parents. Do not forget that all disordered parents once were children who grew up. Children with psychopathic traits may show these behaviours in early childhood. Statistics tell us that one in a hundred children have psychopathic traits. Signs include:

- Emotional coldness - lack of empathy. The child may be able to appear polite but does not react emotionally when others are sad or upset.

- Lying or deceptive behaviour, manipulative. The child knows how to manipulate people to get what they want.

- Fearlessness. The child does not accept punishment for anything they did; they feel no guilt.

- Sometimes they also have a hair-trigger temper.

Also, read the more detailed information about the instrument CPTI coming soon.

Another behaviour that hurts a lot to think about and which children with psychopathic traits sometimes engage in is animal cruelty. They may nail up a cat in its paws on a tree trunk and let it hang there until it dies… Yes, if such behaviour occurs in your surroundings, the alarm bells should ring loudly!

It is important to seek contact with a specialist concerning children who exhibit behaviours as above. They need help in a very early stage to learn the social codes and morals, as they lack the inner emotional compass. That is the compass that supports most of us by showing us the way in life.

"Anna," from a previous piece in this book, tells the following after breaking up with Mårten: *I feel that I give my children a good upbringing, it's not certain that they will pass on his psychopathic traits. These children need to learn that if you pull the cat by the tail, it hurts, and if you let your friends down, you will lose them. Psychopathic individuals cause so much misery to so many people that everything must be done to prevent that development within a child. I don't think any biological parent is good for a child. Children with psychopathic traits should perhaps be moved from their home environment and come to an advantageous foster home. Mårten was not a whole person. His childhood wasn't easy. If he had got the chance to grow up in a healthier family, he might have been a different person."*

Psychopathic Traits within Children – The Instrument CPTI

CPTI = Child Problematic Traits Inventory is an instrument used by preschool teachers and other instructors to assess psychopathic traits in children. It is important to raise awareness about the following regarding a child who constantly gives many dilemmas to solve.

- Likes change and that things happen all the time

- Seldom expresses sympathy for others

- Often has difficulties with awaiting his/her turn

- Usually does not seem to share other's joy and sorrow

- Lies often to avoid problems

- Seems to do certain things just for the thrill of it

- Seems to see himself/herself as superior compared to others

- Never seems to have a bad conscience for things that he/she has done

- Often lies to get what he or she wants

- Provides himself/herself with different things very fast and eagerly

- Often seems to be completely indifferent when other children are upset

- Often do things without thinking ahead

- Does not become upset when others are being hurt

- Often consumes things immediately rather than saving them

- Seems to lie more than other children of the same age

- Seems to have a great need for change and excitement

- Is seldom remorseful when he/she has done something forbidden

- Is often superior and arrogant towards others

- Does not like waiting

- Often does not seem to care about what other people feel and think

- To get people to do what he/she wants, he/she often find it efficient to con them

- Sometimes seem to completely lack the capability to feel guilt and remorse

- Seems to get bored quickly

- Thinks that he or she is better than almost everyone in almost every aspect

- Never expresses feelings of guilt when he/she has done something forbidden

- Frequent lying seems to be completely normal for him/her

- Does not express guilt and remorse to the same extent as other children of the same age

- Quickly gets tired of things and wants new things to happen all the time

A four-point scale is used as an instrument to gauge the level of psychopathy among children. This is, of course, an instrument to use in collaboration with a specialist. This collaboration can then help professionals to identify an important subgroup of children and young people at risk, with the purpose of making efforts and be able to help these children early. Psychopathic traits have often been shown to be stable over time but can also change during adolescence.

There is no doubt that it is our responsibility to act if a child shows psychopathic traits in childhood. They need to be followed closely throughout the upbringing, and everything should be documented in case a future partner or future children reveals the most incredible information concerning the home situation. Today there is no security for the affected individuals. When new information occurs regarding a person showing these traits as a child, he or she, of course, need support to get right back on track. Closest relatives, such as parents and siblings, probably are the people who will be present in life most frequently, and these people need to have knowledge of the condition. They need to get the best tools there are to make their family member stop hurting others and also themselves. These young people need help very early to see and realise that their behaviour doesn't benefit them in the long run.

If the psychopathy diagnosis is silenced, there is no chance that this can be obtained. We leave the psychopathic person without support and also the family.

Of course, we must be careful not to overdramatise a child's behavioural patterns. To identify psychopathic traits, behaviour patterns should be observed for recurrence for a longer period of time, and nothing should be established earlier than the age of five to six. However, if we do understand that a child may be at risk just by studying the family, it's another story. We must be aware of the fact that most adults suffering from psychopathy have exhibited symptoms since childhood, so when we suspect it, we need to investigate the child's family situation. When or if you find patterns and explanations regarding a child's behaviour, you can start to adjust the environment accordingly and work consciously towards improving the child's behaviour. Do everything you can to prevent or reduce future problems.

Sometimes ignorance and fear within parents, who in fact are well-functional, affect the situation in the wrong way. Say, for example, a child with psychopathic traits caused by discrepancies in the brain is growing up in a family that is really a well-functional one. Unfortunately, the parents lack knowledge and therefore do not understand their child's behaviour. As a consequence of this lack of knowledge, they react with harshness, resistance and strong distaste to the child's emotional coldness and lies. They react with anger. Of, course this may lead to a conflict-filled upbringing for the child, which then possibly reinforces the psychopathic traits as a consequence of the parents' ignorance. With knowledge of the child's disorder, parents may be able to approach the child in a completely different way, hopefully with patience, warmth, explanations, understanding, the correct boundaries and specialist's help. We cannot have a world where people aren't made responsible for their actions, and the child must learn the differences between right and wrong early in life. There is no chance to accomplish this if knowledge regarding the disorder is missing.

If parents and other adults lack knowledge and therefore meet fire with fire, and also use punishment as a regular consequence of child's bad behaviour, the child cannot be helped. Instead, there is a great risk of infecting the child with shame. That is extremely dangerous because suppressed shame sometimes leads to narcissism within a person.

By constantly being exposed to parents' and other adults' aggression and penalties, as consequences for not understanding social codes etc., the child is not able to learn anger management. They must learn right and wrong in other ways.

Talking and explaining is a concept that is entirely given. The same goes for choosing suitable consequences if there are to be consequences. Consequences (not penalties) must be possible to explain to the child, and therefore there must be a connection between cause and effect. Further, a compassionate behaviour shown from adults is what may provide the child with a sense of self-worth and a role model to try to emulate.

How should parents know that their children are at risk if they don't know or understand the children's behaviour? That is where getting the correct diagnosis and expert help becomes crucial. Something that worries me is parents' natural way of defending themselves and their children. We should reflect on how we best can reach through to a parent with the message: *We do see psychopathic traits within your child*. It is probably the absolute most difficult fact to absorb as a parent. If the parents themselves seem to be mentally healthy, however, they would likely accept the truth eventually, and they will realise that the best thing to do is to try to find out as much as possible for the child having a chance of gaining a productive development after all.

Through my job as a teacher, I met a mother who was deep in trouble with her child. Her daughter was lying every day, and it was serious lies indeed. (Also, read about the 'conspirators' coming soon.) The mother was also very worried that her daughter lacked empathy for her siblings and others. The girl's father had been diagnosed with ADHD, and the mother discussed this matter with me. I could sense she was very open to my thoughts about it because she herself had reached the end of the road. She didn't know what to do anymore. In this situation, I mentioned to her that there are diagnoses that are placed into the category of personality disorders. ADHD isn't about fraudulent behaviour. Even though I myself am not in a position where I could diagnose people, I can't just keep quiet when I meet troubled parents who have heard about ADHD and believe that that's the problem. To this mother, this was urgent information, and she accepted it completely. She used it to seek help from experts.

Unfortunately, not all parents react this way. Some parents do not understand that their child's lack of empathy may be a problem, and they also diminish their child's lies and deceptive behaviour by defending him or her. In these cases, parents would never accept my explanations of possible personality disorders or psychopathic traits. However, I will contribute negatively to the child's wellbeing and our society if I exclude these matters from the conversation regarding the child. I must at least tell them that at school, we have experienced a lack of empathy for quite some time now or had a troublesome period of lying on the child's behalf. That it is a serious matter and we are in urgent need of cooperation with parents and the family centre to steer children's development in another direction.

Child's Withdrawing

I want to describe a pattern within children that I have noticed and that, in my experience, also is a clear warning signal. It is about the children who have difficulties regarding social interaction in a way that causes them to withdraw from social gatherings… *"because they are right."* These are children who prefer not to spend time with others and certainly not if the interaction is not based on their own terms. They are having difficulties listening to others and getting along, and they become extremely upset if they perceive they are being stepped on their toes. It may be enough to be trampled on one toe. The problem magnifies, and they withdraw to lick their wounds. It is only themselves who is right, and everyone else is wrong, and they can not apologise to anyone. Others are just wrong constantly.

They are doing things in their own way, no matter how strange it gets when they are supposed to be together with friends. An example may be when everyone else is going for a swim at *Frog's beach*, except for Andrew, who is going to *Toad's beach* for his swim. In fact, he also thinks that those who choose to stay at Frog's beach, that is, all the others, are little less intelligent people. Yet your perception of Andrew's behaviour is strangely contradictory. Poor self-confidence and uncertainly sometimes shine through if you watch him through a magnifying glass.

I have seen people growing up to be narcissistic adults, and they showed this anti-social behaviour as children. If we look closer, there are, in fact, strong warning signals for narcissism, that eventually may become one driving factor within a psychopathic individual. It's just that we don't want to embrace the fact when it comes to children, as, of course, they are individuals still in the formative stages of development.

However, shutting our eyes to the problem won't benefit children in this very situation, nor can we smooth it over by saying that the behaviour is caused by "his genes" or that "he's still only a child." I can not stress enough on giving them ALL the help they require to learn the social codes as early as possible in life, so they can improve and grow as human beings in a positive manner. They need to learn that all people are different and do have different ways of thinking. And that it's not dangerous to have a discussion. They need to learn to say that they are sad instead of getting angry or withdraw. They need to know that it is important to be an individual who is interested in other people and how *they feel*. They probably don't know anything about that. These children also need help to see the grayscale because not everything is black or white in the world. Furthermore, we still are living in a world where most people are good people, not evil. In my opinion, this probably must be emphasised to these children quite frequently. Being overly suspicious may make us sick. And why not sometimes point out that the whole thing can be taken lightly and that taking everything so very seriously all the time doesn't always benefit you. Then there is also the incredibly strong antidote called the *sense of humour*. Joking and laughing a lot gives us a taste of life in the true sense of the word. They need to have fun sometimes, so they know how genuine joy feels, how to appreciate it and learn how they can create this feeling by themselves. Some children may not be able to do this as a consequence of biological defects, but it won't hurt to be a positive role model. According to my notion, the people I refer to while talking about psychopathy and narcissism in this piece, have suffered from a lack of genuine joy in life. They have had sarcastic humour instead. These people have been able to laugh, sometimes even loudly. But the more I think about it, the stronger the feeling gets that they lack the warm and genuine feeling of joy most of us are able to experience from the depths of our hearts. Teaching children the social codes is extremely important, and collective, kind-hearted humour from the depth of our hearts is a five-star social code!

Another answer to these children's problems is the absence of the power of action in a controlled manner. Everything that happens isn't badly meant by other people. Talking and sorting out misunderstandings or expressing one's feelings is of great importance. Teach children ways to tackle problems immediately and to seek solutions immediately, and ask for advice. Children with the above attitude, namely that they are constantly negatively affected by everything and everyone all the time without being able to do anything about it, may need very regular help redirecting these thoughts. A good role model who solves problems instead of feeling sorry for oneself month after month doesn't hurt either, as you understand. To be a good role model also means not to say bad things about other people all the time. Of course, it's okay to talk about it if you're hurt by someone else, but that is a different context.

The fact that you've made mistakes once and a while is also a good thing to admit. As an adult, it's very relieving to be strong enough to say: *"Well, it is my fault that I got a parking ticket. I'll sort it out and then it will be soon forgotten,"* and to be able to say this without the feeling of going into pieces is all the more plausible. The opposite may be to see oneself as a victim of external and unfortunate circumstances, get upset at the system regarding parking regulations and try to defend oneself even though it is obvious who made a mistake. Then you feel worse. It also leads to a feeling of being a victim unable to do something about the situation. It is a good thing to influence children's attitude from the beginning of life: *"It's okay to make mistakes, it's okay, and you can influence the situation for the better afterwards, you have the power to do so."* These children also need to know that they shouldn't strike the parking attendant in the face if she is still standing in the parking lot.

Being social is an extremely important protective factor. If you come from a dysfunctional family and don't seek contact outside the family, in the well-functional world where social life is predictable and social codes exist, you may lose a good future. And that's exactly what can happen to children who withdraw. These children do not seek a social life where they can get perspective, support, joy… and much more. They never get to experience all the positive factors from the social world most of us live in. In an isolated world, it is difficult to find solutions to problems. There is a risk that they will remain in a state of feeling sorry for themselves, considering themselves as victims being powerless. They may experience life as more and more difficult as time goes by, and the more difficulties they experience, the more flaws they will "find" within other people, and the darker and more negative their attitude towards the outside world will become. This way, they create an alternative image of reality. A skewed perception of reality makes it difficult to approach people, and the vicious circle is a fact.

A study conducted at a Swedish university has shown that the capacity to *know who you are, where you are going* and *how to collaborate with the environment* seems to be important factors to recover or to avoid falling into continuing problems in life [27].

It is also important to mention the research that has shown that children are born with different temperaments. Some children are naturally more difficult than others to raise. But we must never stop trying, and we should get help if we don't have the strength to do this alone. Understanding caregivers, who know how to show love while setting boundaries in a calm and predictable way, instead of using constant punishment, may affect the child's behaviour in a way that makes the fierce temper fade rather than escalate [28]. All children who develop narcissistic or psychopathic

---

[27]https://www.forskning.se/2017/09/14/insatser-kan-motverka-psykisk-ohalsa-vid-aggressivt-antisocialt-beteende/

[28] Pervin, L & Cervone, D (2010) *Personality. Theori and research.* New York: John Wiley and sons.

personalities do not withdraw. Some of them have a forward behaviour or more openly aggressive behaviour and may show far and wide that they are the best, the strongest, the smartest...

In both cases, an advantageous upbringing, one based on knowledge regarding one's children, of course, is a significant part of the solution. Accepting help and guidance by professionals if needed is also important, as is a favourable and open collaboration with school and daycare.

Unfortunately, problems will turn up if a child is narcissistic as a consequence of the parent being narcissistic. A narcissistic parent is too busy with oneself to be able to give their child a healthy upbringing. He or she will not be interested in gathering knowledge regarding children's development. Children are something that simply only exist. Or not. A narcissistic parent would not recognise the need for help from professionals, as he or she manages the parenting very well on their own, and at last, school and daycare are probably full of idiots who knows nothing and lack even the basic understanding of looking after a child.

The Conspirators

Let us make ourselves aware of one more kind of children who, in the long run, are at risk of not being welcome in a friendship nor in the labour market. I'm talking about the *Conspirators*. Many of us have met them. They are often girls, and it seems like they are easily bored with life. Of course, then, to make life more thrilling for a day or a month, they find or create something to get excited about. It may be telling a lie to a friend or about a friend who then sets the ball rolling. These children are usually very good liars, so when this other person starts to defend himself or herself, this one single lie may grow into an increasing number of lies or into more serious ones.

A situation may also be *created*, for example, by inviting a friend over and offer a gift. When the "dear friends" arrive at school the day after, and the gift is brought - the trouble begins. A teacher is told:

- She has stolen it from me!

- I really don't believe Ann would do such a thing.

- Yes, she did! She was at my place yesterday, and I had it in my room. Look, my initials are on the backside!

If teachers and caregivers don't cooperate to put a stop to this behaviour in youth, it may turn out devastating for people around and also for the "drama queen" herself. The reputation of not being a reliable person will follow her.

If such a child isn't believed, she (or he, but mostly she) may make herself the victim or go straight up to the next level of aggressive behaviour and lies. To see through it to reveal the lies becomes absolutely crucial then. Avoiding to step down as a consequence of the child's aggression and accusations that may follow when you confront these children, will be challenging. However, it must be shown that there is no painless way out of it. *You will eventually get caught, so why not just stop it. Now.*

If we fail in youth, these girls as teenagers may start lying about, for example, men. A grown-up man is very vulnerable to lies regarding sexuality. Everyone around gets suspicious when a man is claimed to look at young girls, touching a young girl or have said something to her, even if he never did. Just think about it for a moment. Often men *are* hurting women. Yes, we have seen it in this book and in fact, *everywhere else* too. So many men have, in fact, really been hurting women, probably for thousands and thousands of years, that when an innocent, decent man is accused, he really is suspected. What if it would be your boyfriend, husband, friend or son, who was exposed to this kind of evil behaviour? If this turns out very badly, together with spreading rumours, it may force a man to move away with his family.

This is when the importance of documentation comes in. School staff and others really need to document carefully, with dates and all, because often you can see these traits early in life. When many situations *in different contexts* are put down to paper, a pattern will appear. Also, if a boy seems to show unhealthy behaviour towards girls, it must also be put down to paper. Keeping documentation is crucial in these cases, in fact, in all cases in this book.

If you know about a child who behaves like this, try to make yourself aware of the problem and do what you can to help the child out of it as early in the child's life as possible. If they don't learn this in their youth, they will be at risk of falling on their own grip later in life. It is important that they receive *understanding*, understanding for the fact that it will affect them later.

Some of these young conspirators will also develop an unhealthy way of getting ahead in the labour market:

A teacher becomes exhausted from work and stays at home for four weeks. Meanwhile, a young locum tenens replaces her for these weeks. The teacher is then receiving the chance to come back to work slowly, to make it. The locum tenens is therefore staying in the class, and the teacher works with small groups of students from her class in a small room on another floor of the school.

On the first day back at work, the teacher experiences that she is welcomed back by everyone except her replacer. She presents herself to her young temporary replacer, and yes, Siberia is a warmer place on earth, really. Then the breakdown begins.

The teacher, weakened from many tough years at work, now gets to hear how well functional the class has been since she left (which isn't true according to students and parents). The teacher won't even get the chance to explain her point of view without getting interrupted. With the argument that the replacer should get the chance to win authority in the class, the ordinary teacher isn't allowed in the classroom. This gives her replacer a great chance to steer the class into whichever direction she ever wants.

The earlier beloved ordinary teacher experiences that her students are negatively set to join her lessons. This goes on for several weeks. Then, it suddenly gets better. The students show up for a few weeks and learn a lot in these small groups. The temporary replacer sends text messages, which are necessary as communication during the working day, because the teacher, as said, isn't allowed to enter her classroom. The text messages now include smilies and hearts, "Now, let's solve this TOGETHER ♡ !" The teacher is happy about the fact that her replacer finally seems to have understood the great importance of and need for help in the class.

One day the replacer comes downstairs to the teacher's temporary room to say that the class really is in need of two teachers, that she already has told the principal about it, and that it would be good if the teacher told him the same. The teacher has known about the great needs of this large class for several years, so yes, of course, she repeats it to the principal. She also tells him that it is now much easier to cooperate with the temporary replacer.

Then suddenly, it stops. Suddenly we are back at square one. Students won't show up in the teacher's temporary classroom. No more nice text messages. It turns out that the replacer now has signed her employment contract for staying the rest of the semester.

After this date, the teacher and also another well-educated teacher are bullied out of the class. The locum tenens clearly tries to boost her self-confidence at the other teacher's expense. The students who still want to join their former beloved teacher's lessons are at risk of being bullied by their classmates. With manipulation, lies and hidden messages, the class has been turned against those well-educated teachers, who the young locum tenens believes are threats to her authority. Witch-hunting is a fact in this situation, and the former teacher is forced by choice to leave her class to survive psychologically. Now, we may ask ourselves how a young non-educated locum tenens can succeed bullying two well-educated teachers out of the classroom. It really is unbelievable! But this is a true story.

...

Later the teacher found out that her replacer was one of these children, back in school - one of the conspirators, who wasn't stopped. She had a way to get away with things by not saying them straight out, so it was difficult to really accuse her of something. It was also easy for her to just lie, manipulate or say that she simply had forgotten about things. I guess it would have been easier to teach her the difference between right and wrong in an earlier stage of life. Don't we instead want our children to be good-hearted, wise and independent in a good way? Let's make some efforts then. We need to meet them with warmth, listening and love but also very, very firm frameworks.

Several of the staff at school and also the principal eventually understood what had been going on. The principal had for a long time called the problems "communication difficulties," "misunderstandings," and "cooperation difficulties," and all this time, he tried to force these areas to function. Unfortunately, he realised the actual situation way too late. There was no chance to make it work, of course, because one of the entities did not have honest intentions.

You can recognise these situations from the answers you get from the managers:

- She keeps on telling me that it goes so well in the class since she came. I'm not even allowed to finish what I want to say. Students and parents tell me otherwise, but she just goes on.

    - Isn't it good for you to hear that it's going well in the classroom?

- She diminishes me in front of the class. I guess I have to argue, too, then? To defend myself?

    - No, you shouldn't bring disagreements up in front of the class.

- She keeps feeding me how well she is doing. Everything positive that happens is her merit, and everything is solved since she came to the class. But when she fails, she blames me in front of the students and the parents, even if I had nothing to do with it.

    -Can you give her that? – she wants to be good at this.

- Yes, but I'm having a hard time when it comes to playing nasty and when it gets mean.

    -What you are telling me about her isn't so nice either, is it?

- She lied to me straight in the face twice yesterday.

    -No, we shouldn't believe that we've got mean people in the building. You are having problems with communication, cooperation and there may be misunderstandings.

166

- What part of "standing up for each other to the level of 100 % in front of the students" did she miss when we talked about it yesterday?

- Maybe you have different views of what it means to stand up for each other to the level of 100 % in front of the students?

This had been going on for three months when the teacher got her face ripped off the class photo and finally gave up. It's like the managers have their eyes open without being able to see. It seems as if personality disordered people or "conspirators" have this effect on them. Disordered people know how to manipulate others, and they are well aware of how to act to take advantage of group processes. However, when a witch's bonfire is burning and you are begging for help, but no one is around to put the fire out – well there is a way to consider it, namely: *There is always a limit that shows when people around you just don't deserve your attention anymore. Maybe it's time for you to take care of yourself for a while instead of keeping on fighting?*

Now, who has the most serious problems in the long run? The teacher or the conspirator? Will the replacer be recommended for further employments when this story surfaces? And stories from other workplaces add as well?

Again: If you know a young girl who acts this way (or a boy), try to make yourself aware of the problem, keep documentation, do what you can to put a stop to it as early in the child's life as possible. If they don't learn as young, they may end up as victims as a consequence of their own behaviour.

Children with Misleading Diagnosis

According to research, there is a connection between ADHD and psychopathy. If we treat children with diagnosis ADHD incorrectly, there is a risk for psychopathy to develop within them.

Recently I spoke to one of my colleagues about these personality disorders. She exclaimed: *"People talk about ADHD, people talk about Autism, but this is never mentioned!"* I've experienced the same thing. We *are* talking about ADHD and Autism. We also talk to each other about children who are having difficulties in their homes. But the knowledge of personality disorders - the subject of this book - is lacking. This is serious, as these children and their parents are difficult to discover as it is.

Children having difficulties at home sometimes react with symptoms that are similar to the symptoms that are known regarding ADHD. It has for a long time been known that some children are misdiagnosed because symptoms are similar. According to statistics, medication for ADHD are given to more children than the number research found out are having the diagnosis [29]. In that case, children receive and are given strong medication against something they do not have. Some of these might be children growing up under very harsh circumstances, hidden inside the walls at home. They, therefore, react, which is healthy, but instead of us understanding their behaviour, they are blunted with medication. That is a great betrayal. Not a deliberate betrayal, though a serious one.

I know it can be difficult to spot other underlying causes. More is required from an investigation to discover the children's home conditions and genetics than what is required to discover ADHD and then explain a child's difficulties by that diagnosis. Some of these misdiagnosed children may be children who do have parents lacking the ability to provide their child with the security and structure they need at the beginning of life. Some of them may have a

---

[29]https://utforskasinnet.se/5-tecken-pa-att-du-uppfostrar-narcissistiska-barn/

parent with a personality disorder or be suffering from one themselves. So, what is what exactly? How difficult it may seem, we must find ways to improve ourselves, so the research and statistics equal at a higher rate. Get better at distinguishing these disorders and diagnoses. We will never be able to succeed in all these cases of difficulties that arise, but for each case that is resolved in a correct way, it's a great success. The child then has a chance of being helped into a mentally healthy path in life, get explanations and support. We may then have stopped a destructive legacy in that particular family chain.

Another thing that is extremely well worth knowing is that there seems to be a connection between ADHD and psychopathy [30]. It is known that a small proportion of children having the diagnosis of ADHD develop psychopathy. It is a connection which researchers want to learn more about, and it's being worked on. The connection could be as follows:

"Children with ADHD are at risk of developing anti-social traits due to the lack of attention and impulse control.

---

[30] Kreis, M, Hoff. H.A, Belfrage, H & Hart, S (2016) *Psykopati.* Studentlitteratur.

It is considered that the risk of psychopathy increases significantly if the environment does not correctly assess the condition, but instead punishes the child for things he or she cannot help." [31]

To teach parents and school staff, in fact, everyone who meet children privately or at work, a "low-arousal approach" may be an important factor for these children. Criticism regarding this approach has been heard. However, often, one has misunderstood the purpose of it and how it should be implemented, says Bo Hejlskov, author on this subject [32].

The low-arousal approach is about finding out the causes, arranging environments and setting boundaries in a way that doesn't involve penalties. Those who have read Bo Hejlskovs books and managed to connect the content to this book understand that this can be a very important factor to children with ADHD, who cannot always control their bodies and their behaviour. Especially after reading the previous quote. It is worth repeating the fact that punishment

---

[31]https://www.psykologiguiden.se/rad-och-fakta/symtom-och-besvar/personlighetsstorningar/psykopati
[32] Heilskov, Bo (2014) *Beteendeproblem i skolan*. Natur och kultur.

for things we can't help or control is, in many cases, totally devastating.

Considering the fact that a small proportion of children having the diagnosis ADHD develop psychopathy or psychopathic traits, the diagnosis of ADHD does not have to be "wrong." It's just that it is something more – or *becomes* something more due to incorrect knowledge, attention and treatment. Maybe the fact that the child has developed psychopathy *as well* will never be established. The child has already "received a diagnosis" - ADHD. And then he or she becomes a parent, without psychopathy being treated (as well as it can be) or documented. When they have grown up, as we have learned, it almost becomes impossible to establish the diagnosis, and by that fact, help won't get through. I, myself, have experienced a situation where a parent exhibited crystal clear psychopathic traits through terrible behaviour but got away with everyone mentioning, *"He is diagnosed ADHD."*

However, it will also be highly wrong to all the other children and adults diagnosed with ADHD and other illnesses, for that matter, since they are being confused/burdened with the picture of them having psychopathic traits such as deceptive behaviour and emotional coldness. Children with ADHD do not make up fraudulent plans. They are just impulsive and cannot at the moment control themselves. We should be able to learn to distinguish one thing from another and then provide the correct support and treatment.

With the knowledge that some adult psychopathic individuals as well are having the diagnosis ADHD, and with the knowledge that ADHD is a genetically inherited diagnose, we should pay extra attention. Children with ADHD may be at risk of developing psychopathy if the surroundings misjudge the condition and raise the child with punishments for things that couldn't be controlled. Then think for a minute about a psychopathic parent who lacks the moral barriers and also only has an interest in himself alone… I have heard with my own ears an undoubtedly psychopathic parent "raising" his child. His children are at risk for growing up with huge damage done to them. His son was diagnosed with ADHD. When parents suffering from both ADHD and psychopathy raise a child also having ADHD inherited, I believe this may be a very significant breeding ground for psychopathy.

When looking for causes regarding the issue of heredity or environment, it is interesting to know the following information from a twin study conducted by Lichtenstein, Eley and Moffitt:

Regarding *aggressive anti-social behaviour*, one sees a significant genetic influence. Regarding *non-aggressive anti-social behaviour*, there is more of an environmental connection and explanation to the state. This knowledge may help us a bit along the way if we seek explanations for children's behaviour.

School and Daycare Are Important Institutions

In school, staff sometimes become suspicious regarding children's home situation without this information coming to light. A social secretary I spoke to told me that fewer notifications are coming to their desks than actually is the case. We should know that each person with a notification is obligated to report the concerns, and if not doing so, one may be convicted of misconduct according to the law. If social services and/or other authorities are already involved but concerns for the child remain, a new notification of concern must be submitted. Otherwise, it may also be considered misconduct. Despite this, we understand that there may be a great estimated number of unknown cases regarding these concerns.

Fear is one explanation for this. When dealing with personality disordered parents, insecurity often takes hold of the staff as these parents may prove to be threatening. A number of years ago, I myself was involved in a meeting where both principal and curator at a school did everything they could to reduce staffs suspicions to avoid reporting to the social services. They felt that it was too uncomfortable, and the feeling I got was that they were waiting for the child to graduate and start high school. It was only one semester left… Then it would be someone else's problem.

If the parents are threatening, there is at least a chance that problems will be revealed. If they instead are manipulative, the whole story may be missed, as everything becomes too strange and contradictory to be suspected or explained. We must all be helped to find courage. School or daycare's perception or opinion in the case may be crucial to a child's future. The fear of reporting concerns to social services could be reduced if no one needs to sign their name. The school or school health care is the one taking on the responsibility; no names of private persons should be revealed if possible.

Fear is a fact, and I do not want to know how many children have been left to suffer because of it. Testimony, if that comes up, is also needed to be done in a group if possible. Help each other with cases like these in schools and in daycare, so you can stand up together and be strong. Do everything to make it easier for information to arrive at the right place. No rules in the world could possibly be more important than that. Children should not have to long for their childhood to be over with, waiting for being grown enough to finally leave home and escape their circumstances.

Do not forget that an outside story may be crucial for the outcome of the case. The psychologically healthy parent's story is at risk of being diminished as he or she is seen as one of two equal opponents in a family affair. If witnesses from outside the family, for example, a group of teachers, are willing to testify, that may then determine the outcome of the case. It is then important to also have documentation, with testimonies, events, details and dates. These people will probably be heroes also for future generations. They may become the people who changed *everything*.

Maybe you think it's all about exposing narcissistic and psychopathic parents and that we must have a diagnosis if we are to be believed. Yes, a diagnosis would be desirable because then there is at least a small chance that the suitable treatment reaches the disordered person. It would also mean that we would get information in order to help the children in a suitable way. Maybe, you are thinking that we can't walk around saying that people are psychopathic. To fully reveal somebody as personality disordered, we need an investigation and a diagnosis. We can not force people into doing this. In most cases, we will never really know. However, a diagnosis does not have to be required to act in the best interest of the child. If we know a lot about these defects within parents, how they show, and we actually see and understand that children get badly infected with the same, it will be very wrong if the discussion is to end with the issue whether the parent is psychopathic or not. *It's the behaviour that leads to the damage, not "the diagnosis."*

If relatives and family members tell their story, we must reflect on the behaviour and try to see through their version. This kind of game, the chessboard game, isn't okay for children or adults. It must be done right there. If you're still feeling critical, you need to look at the other side of the coin. Do you dare to ignore that there are signs of psychopathy within a parent? Which is the best to do if we ought to think about the children? That you open up to your fears and take a closer look, or that you shut your eyes as hard as you can?

To the Girl with the Phone Call

If the children don't receive help from adults, it's just to hope that they themselves can take matters into their own hands. The girl in the horrible, destructive conversation with her psychopathic father had come to a state where she would have to save herself. Her mother is one of the two women who told me about the locked position. If you, little girl, ever read this and happen to recognise yourself, *I cheer for you!* You may not yet know how correctly you have acted. Continue to follow the knowledge of life that makes you put a stop to it. If your dad is going in one direction concerning behaviour, opinions, actions, yes, anything, make sure to walk in the other direction. It's probably right in most situations. Keep thinking for yourself and about yourself, as you do today. Get on living and gaining new impressions, knowledge and perspectives. It is another world out there, significantly different from what you are used to. Try not to miss that. Let people in to help you when you need help. I know that your mother supports you in your own choices.

Hand on Heart

"Our culture is full of narcissistic influences that numb us to the depths of the problems we face. To fight back, we need strong, real selves that are capable of transcending

mere self-interest. When we understand where self-esteem really comes from and make a commitment to raising healthy children – when this becomes our number one priority- we will have turned the corner towards a better world."

Sandy Hotchkiss.

With your hand on your heart, how many people reading this book have heard, seen or in another way known or suspected that destructive acts are going on within a family? Act, if possible. Contact authorities if the situation seems to be a bit too dangerous to act yourself. Authorities may have difficulties acting without evidence. There is a risk that they will meet a completely different parent than the one you have seen. Don't forget about the manipulation and lies that may appear. If there is evidence, save it.

Humans often have the ability to avoid discomfort. We want to protect ourselves and live our lives in peace if we can. But, we are in the same boat. The name of this big boat is *Society*. *We* are the Society, and it is a hell of a boat! We may imagine that we are protecting ourselves by not acting when something is wrong, but instead, we endanger our children's lives.

Now, join me for a mind game:

179

Imagine all of the children who are growing up right now in destructive families, where their personality is triggered every day into an "evil" personality. Perhaps becoming just the way their parents are or worse.

Then imagine that maybe a hundred people know there is something going on, but they are beating around the bush. School staff, relatives, neighbours, the coach… You are one of them. Nobody acts. Neither do you. Now imagine that the children grow up, and as quite expected, they have developed in the narcissistic or psychopathic direction due to the failure of the first four barriers that should function as protection. Do you remember?

- The disordered personality parent discovers that something is wrong and acts by seeking help.

- The other adult in the family – the partner – receives information and knowledge and realises what the family is actually affected by. And then dares to act.

- Some from outside the family, a relative, social authorities, police, nursing staff or school get a view of patterns and act.

- That the law as a result steps in to protect children.

Nor have these children succeeded in the fifth and final point:

- If none of these "protective barriers" work well, then only the children can save themselves. It is far from all children who succeed.

Now imagine that one of these, now a grown child, is out one evening, looking for a partner, manipulative, glowing from perfection. Then comes your son or daughter. He or she, your dear child, exclaims in thought:

- *Oh, such an amazing person! I've just got to have this wonderful person in my life!*

I repeat: Society is a hell of a boat. We all are sitting in it. No one wants to be exposed. As said; We spit, and we swear when someone is cheated, beaten, raped or murdered, but we aren't always there to prevent it. We believe that we will be safe from not acting. This is our children's present and future fellow human beings growing up. Lay your hand on your heart and say if this is untrue.

The Bystander Effect

We have many huge problems on the boat Society. In this world of great human self-preoccupation, the preoccupation that partly leads to narcissism, all of us may get in trouble much sooner than we might believe and that in a different context from that of personality disorders. People's fear of inconveniences makes our society unsafe in so many ways. The by-stander effect [33] shows us that we follow other people's example, even if we deep within our hearts know what we are doing is wrong:

A man is on the ground outside a library in a big town. He is holding his arms on his belly, and you can see that he is in pain. His voice is weak, but once and a while, you can hear "Help." People who see him pass by. Some of them slow their footsteps down for a second, but soon they keep on walking at the same speed as before noticing him. For twenty minutes, hundreds of people pass by him until finally, one person walks towards him and asks how he is feeling. Once this person has stopped, many follow his example.

---

[33] http://www.youtube.com/watch?v=OSsPfbup0ac

Now, both you and I may think: *"I would never have passed, of course, I would have stopped and called for help!"* Yes, we really want to believe that regarding ourselves. But with the fact that hundreds of people just walk by this suffering man, it is probably wrong to take for granted that we ourselves doubtless would have stopped. Isn't it a fact that we really, really want to avoid getting involved in inconveniences, events that may mean trouble? Isn't that so that we want our lives to continue without interruption? Are we searching for excuses for not getting involved? Is it a fact that the more people that are present, the less responsibility lies within each and one of us?

If we imagine for a second that it is ourselves, or maybe our grown-up child who is lying there, with unbearable stomach pain, without being able to breathe, and with the conviction that this may be the last day in life, and hundreds of citizens look at you and just pass by... How would we feel when we experience such a thing? Would we ever get over it?

The fact is that this isn't unusual human behaviour. It might not seem so strange that our society can be experienced as unsafe and cold. We can't count on people to help us when we really need it.

A similar event happened to a friend of mine. He collided with a moose. The car was afterwards ready for the junkyard, and he was so lucky to survive! There was another driver right behind him, and I took for granted that he or she saw what had happened. Though, this driver passed. When one driver has chosen to pass, it is also easier for other drivers to follow the example. *"He passed. I can do it too. More cars are coming. Why should I have the trouble? Maybe they know something about it which I don't."*

I, myself, have also participated in this insane behaviour as a young child. In my book, *Safe Harbour*, I tell my readers about a boy in my class that, just like me, was bullied. I remember one occasion of him being treated like a ragdoll. He screamed *"No, No, No!"* but none of us classmates did anything to help him. The fear we felt of needing to replace him made us paralysed. The question is – would anybody at all be at risk of becoming a ragdoll if we had been united. If we only had been united... And it also would have been a good thing if the teachers ever would have chosen to see what was going on. As a teacher, I today know that with all that bullying that was going on in that class – it's just not possible to not see it for six years. Not possible.

Of course, we have to choose occasions to use our civil courage. We shouldn't go in between and try to stop an ongoing fight with knives included. At least not without a great deal of help. But we can do *something*. We can call the police. Now, the question is how scared we are of getting involved. If we have the time to think a few months ahead, we might see ourselves as a witness in the meaning of the law. At the mere thought of a courtroom, we might turn around and walk away without acting.

Is it that we sometimes must be prepared to act if we want to live in a safe society? In all matters. Can we really expect that *"someone else will do something about it"* every time? No matter if it is a car accident or a child needing help from social services, or an abused neighbour wife.

If we as parents repeatedly tell our children, *"Don't interfere with other people's lives,"* as soon it gets a bit uncomfortable, is it then so strange that the by-stander effect exists? If the younger generation sees their adult role models pass a suffering man on the street or pass a driver who just collided with a moose... Is it then so strange that bullying is going on in our schools? That children avoid getting involved when someone is bullied? They learn from the generation before to avoid inconveniences at any cost.

I don't think that it will be enough if just a few of us choose the brave way of life. There have to be many of us. If there are to be many of us, our society will probably have become a much safer place within one generation. Or a half. Or even within a month of time. This afternoon.

When the man on the street was on the ground, paralysed from pain, it really was enough with one single person stepping forward for others to line up – and do the right thing. Most of us know within ourselves how to act for the best in most cases. I can not imagine a child passing by a hurting man without showing concern, looking upon the parent with a question in their face. What do I do then, as a parent? Do I say *"sch"* to my child and pass, or do I stop, bring someone else that I have next to me in the crowd and show my child that the right thing to do is to *act*? Imagine all parents telling and showing their children that acting is the right thing to do. Will then anyone ever need to be afraid to put an end to bad situations? Will then anyone ever be afraid of becoming anyone's ragdoll? Won't we then see a safer future for our children, grandchildren and their fellow human beings?

Bright Footprints

"The world needs to be lit up in many places. Luckily there are many of us who can light our lanterns."

A strong desire I have is to leave bright footprints from me and my time on earth. Perhaps we often forget about it in the everyday stress which we as humans have created. But I see you, my friends. You, who think in the same way. It can be about donating a penny to a charity fund, make an eco-friendly choice, bring warm smiles to children's faces the grocery store – such smiles they can recall when they go to bed at night - helping a person who is being bullied or a child in need of security.

One of the threats to this is not a lack of human goodness, but we are often sitting in the 21st-century jet plane. We do not have the time to stop, and the bystander effect is also in our way if we aren't aware of it.

But still, try to do it sometimes. Leave a bright footprint. And do not forget to show, tell and explain to your children how, when and why you leave your bright footprints. Maybe we will get the chance to leave the earth in a better condition than it was when we arrived and with growing generations who also work together to make the world a better place than it was when they arrived.

"One random act of kindness at a time, will as time passes, change the world."
Luckily there are many of us who can light our lanterns!

Some Ingredients that Missed Me – Important Things for Building Self-Esteem

Now, let's talk about self-esteem and some of the areas that are important to be aware of as a parent.

Knowledge and Objective Thinking

I tell: In my family, dad's words were law. He never said it out loud, but that is probably the case regarding narcissistic people. With his strong appearance, there was no question about it. We never questioned him. His perspective was the right one, and it also became our perspective. The thought of him being wrong probably never struck us. He often said bad things about other people. Everything was black or white. A grayscale did not exist, that is seeing situations from different perspectives. He decided what his opinion was. We never reasoned about anything. He was like our family's dictator. We did not create any own thoughts or own knowledge about anyone or anything.

I want to establish: It is of great importance that we share our time and knowledge with our children, knowledge that they can use to analyse phenomena they'll be exposed to. Teach them to think about things from different perspectives. In time they will extend and increase their wisdom and knowledge all by themselves, meeting the outside world.

Children need to learn to stand up for something they believe in but also listen to others. They need to be aware of the fact that we are living in a world where we have or should have the right to our own interpretations, thoughts, beliefs and opinions. If we teach them to see things from different angles, they might be able to reveal the family's dictator being wrong once and a while. That might save them from major troubles.

Maybe I'm simplifying the complicated world, which we all usually end up in with these personality disorders present. However, someone or something had made the phonecall-girl think a bit further regarding her father. Also, I did that in time.

As a parent, showing coldness to other people and placing them in black and white boxes may, of course, be a devastating factor. I have seen children actually being sent out of their homes to look for flaws within other people so that parents can be confirmed they were right all along: *"He is a worthless man." "He is good, she is bad, and that's the way it is."* Sometimes children get started on their parents' strong reactions when they, for example, come home from school and tell more about the person, who has now become their object of hatred. The child feels strengthened by the fact that the parents are standing on his or her side for once, really listening, and soon children will search for this attention.

Standing up against parents' attitudes and opinions on various issues, surely, are difficult in these homes, and children continue standing up for their parents... unless... other people they meet in life try to reach through to them, with a wide-open way of seeing people and events teach them to see nuances in everything around them.

Thinking ahead, if they don't receive help, it's not too far to think that serious cooperation difficulties may arise in children's future professional lives and love lives, along with problems such as depression or abuse as a possible result of this inability. The child is simply brought up to be irritated with other people and to look for flaws within others just to explain things that are happening around them. And this will make... who... happy?

Instead, try to soften the children, teach them not to take everything too serious all the time. Teach them not to judge other people too fast. They have to know that most people still are good people in this world, even though they are not good enough to meet "parent's standard."

The feeling of freedom that you'll miss in life if you lack the ability to experience acceptance in heart and soul will lead to lacking the feeling of joy and happiness.

To See Oneself

I tell: I clearly remember how the rest of us overlooked our own joy when we watched movies or a program on TV. We sat there watching dad's reactions to what we saw. If he laughed and was satisfied, we were too. We did not watch for our sake. We did not sit there with our own perceptions of the film. Instead, we lived fully through dad. We saw everything through his eyes, the way we perceived him seeing things.

We also saw ourselves through his eyes. We thought about ourselves as being what he explained we were. The way we thought he perceived us, that way we became.

I did not experience myself as something good. I was no one to be noticed. It was not just dad. I guess there are different ways to react as a child if you are overlooked by, to you, the most important person in the world. You don't get help to build self-esteem, and you, therefore, feel that you're nobody. In my family, there was sibling bullying going on, physically and mentally, and I was the "weak one." Sibling bullying as a concept is something I only recently came to know there is a term for it. Back in the 80's, it wasn't noticed, and maybe it isn't today either. Siblings are fighting, you know…

However, my teenage friends noticed what was going on at home wasn't an ordinary sibling quarrel. It was bullying, constantly ongoing. At school, I did not succeed in defending myself either. I had not learned self-respect, I had no value, and therefore I could not demand respect from others.

I want to establish: It is probably not possible to describe the importance of parents really seeing their children and seeing them in a positive manner. Parent's image of the child becomes the child's image of himself/herself. I probably could have handled bullying at school as well as at home if I had been helped to become strong and to feel valued as a person. Instead, I was used by others to step on, others who needed to feel superior.

Something that is important to know is that in a narcissistic home, there is also a parent working very hard with their profession, home and children and yet experiences

193

a constant, very burdensome feeling of being useless. The narcissistic parent probably weighs down more by being present at home than being elsewhere, like a grown-up child to be taken care of.

Do not make your children feel superior to others, but fill your children with a positive image of themselves. Give warmth and love rather than praise for achievements only. Children should learn to care for themselves and feel that life is good, but without getting performance-based self-esteem or becoming narcissistic themselves.

Parents' interest in their children's inner thoughts and feelings as well as giving love and warmth, can not be compensated with anything else in the whole world. Sometimes I have been thinking: *"We had fun sometimes; therefore, I've had a fairly normal childhood."* We went to an amusement park a few times, for example. But it doesn't matter if you go on trips or someone brings you gifts. Without the parent's commitment and willingness to support the children's individuality, there will be no children with self-esteem. A genuine commitment, of course, lies much deeper within a person than trips and presents.

I think dad knew that we lived through him, and if he had wanted to change that, he could have asked us our opinion of the film we watched, for instance. I, nonetheless, was never asked a single question about my thoughts of anything. Ever. From this experience of my dad, I as a child learned that other people are more important than me. As a teenager and young adult, I took on responsibility for everybody being satisfied, for example at parties. Even if it wasn't my party. I didn't enjoy myself as my first priority. I was worried about everyone else, so no one felt lonely.

I would like to add a few lines regarding praise while we're talking about parents *seeing* their children. Love and warmth for a child are more important than praise for achievements. But does that mean that praise isn't important at all? Absolutely not! As adults, we probably know how it may feel sometimes – we focus too much on what we do badly and the things that went wrong, and at least for me, that usually leads to a kind of general anxiety throughout my existence. The times when I get a little praise for something I have done well may help me to feel a little better again. Praise for achievements can, however, be dangerous on a larger scale and especially if warmth and love are missing from the equation. Then children can be doomed to a life with a constant feeling of hollowness, and the only thing that provides temporary relief is to try to surpass oneself in achievements constantly.

Thoughts and Opinions

I tell: I remember an occasion when we had an outdoor recreation day at school, skating. I was about eight years old. There weren't seats in the bus for all children to sit down, so we stood pressed together like sardines. Sharp skates stuck out of plastic bags.

Perhaps I was thinking too far ahead at the time, but I reacted to this and thought that it was an inappropriate way to drive us home from school. I said that it was a life-threatening way to travel by bus. Unfortunately, dad heard what I said. His words got stuck in my mind. With the most condescending tone and the most condescending facial expression I'd ever heard and seen, he said:

"Ooohhh, have you experienced a life-threatening situation today?"

He shut me up. I didn't say anything more. He crushed my rights and my strength to express my own opinion. I felt that I wasn't allowed to express myself regarding my experiences, things that were going on in my life and create my own opinion about it. Absolutely not in a way that showed any kind of strength. Well, maybe if it had been an opinion that he shared.

Once dad also complained at my voice. He said that I sounded like an aunt of mine and that he didn't like her voice. My opinions weren't allowed, and my voice was disturbing to him. I fell silent.

I want to establish: How do we get confident children if we take away their own thoughts and opinions or diminish the importance of what they are saying when they express their views? Today I know that it isn't a mystery that I didn't grow up to be somebody. It is not a mystery that I experienced total emptiness far into adulthood. I went out into life as a blank sheet strongly influenced by dad. When dad complained about my voice, it did, in a way, shut my voice down for life. I really don't like to talk. I don't like my own voice. But I'm writing instead.

Be sure to listen to your child. Take his or her thoughts and opinions seriously, reason with your child. Be calm and avoid inflating situations, be an adult in your decisions and in your treatment of the child but act if you need to (for example, call the bus company).

Will and Interests

I tell: There was no room for our will. Dad ran through life as if tomorrow didn't exist and did everything he wanted to do. He devoted himself every other weekend to hunting, and I remember that mum sometimes just laid on the couch, disappointed with dad. All day. But it always worked out because when dad came home, he knew just how to charm (manipulate) her for a while, so she was all happy again. Then he took her out dancing which he liked too. We, the children in the family, stayed at home. The coming weekends probably looked the same.

When I was a little girl, we lived not too far from the horse stable. It did not matter to dad if we rode. We walked there by ourselves, we walked home by ourselves, and it certainly wasn't dad who washed the riding clothes! It was my first spare time activity as a child. One evening dad said:

"It was no fun riding, was it?"

He wanted to put a stop to us riding, and he knew that when he said something with his *complaining tone*, we never expressed ourselves in front of him. We said what he wanted to hear. This was not only my first spare time activity as a child. It also became my last. Many years later, it occurred to me that it might have been because he thought it was too expensive. However, for him to go on hunting trips to Canada was no problem. That too from Sweden!

We had a drum at home, and I remember hitting it a few times. That's when dad decided that playing the drums was an interest of mine. All of a sudden, I was the owner of a drum kit that did not inspire me at all. Then I sat playing with him and his friends until late at night and until I fell asleep with the drumsticks in my hands.

No attention was paid if we didn't meet in one of his interests. He always ruled.

I want to establish: The majority of parents I know do put their children in the first room. One day the children have grown up, moved away from home and then you will have more time to spend on yourself again. I'm not talking about the time parents need to gather new energy once and a while. Being a parent may be very demanding, and being a good parent, you need to think about yourself sometimes.

But not showing interest in one's children and avoid offering them activities that may cheer their lives up, lead them to meet new friends and grow as people, just because you only have time for yourself... Yes, if you want to bring up children who will meet life as blank sheets, this is a part of the recipe. To not even ask them what they want to do.

Attention

I tell: To dad, achievement was one of the most important things in life. He was constantly stressed over his work, which, next to hunting, dancing and music, was his major interest – his own business, which he would never have closed down for the sake of his family. We were there for him, not the other way around. When we sometimes had dinner together, he read the newspaper while eating, and it needed to be quiet around the table. He said that he needed that to calm down and to avoid eating under stress.

Many years later, I can see that he didn't notice us, not even when we were close or when we gathered around him. Seeing us and talking to us couldn't be a better experience than reading a newspaper which he considered was his well-being.

I felt that if it ever was about us, it still was about him. He only apparently wanted to be a good father. As dad grew older and another man started bragging about his grandchildren and what they could do (which in itself is a strange phenomenon), dad also started bragging about what his grandchildren could do. He talked about his grandchildren, who he didn't even know.

I want to establish: As said, achievement was very important to dad. Therefore, I also grew up with performance-based self-esteem, which was difficult to break free from. He never demanded anything from me when it came to schoolwork; he never knew if I had any homework. But, him speaking badly about all these people that he considered weren't good enough, I, of course, understood that it was very important to perform very well if to be accepted in this world. However, I never experienced being someone in dad's eyes despite my accomplishments if I did not turn out to be good at something that he thought was interesting, of course. Things that weren't within his area of interests did not exist. When not giving children attention, they are doomed to be nobody when they see themselves in the mirror.

Ask your children how their day has been. Show interest in their homework and help them if they need help. See them and help them to grow into the individuals they wish to be. Show them that you care, and ask them what they would like. Let them try new things. And most important of all, give them all your warmth, your love and your attention.

Do Not Blame

I tell: My dad had a dream about leaving Sweden and moving to Canada. It was the great wilderness that inspired him. He also had his best friend there.

When I was eight years old, we went to the Canadian Embassy in Stockholm. I remember us three children sitting very still and quiet on a sofa in the corner of the room, and mum and dad sat in armchairs in front of a desk being interviewed. At the end of the interview, the woman raised and walked to our corner of the room. She also wanted to interview us. I was only eight, and I couldn't speak English. We just sat there trying to be polite despite our lack of words. My brother has a severe hearing loss, so he didn't even hear. Mum couldn't speak English either. Thirty-five years later, she still can't.

On the way home, dad felt that it didn't go well. He stopped the car, and he yelled at us. He was angry because we hadn't said anything at the Embassy. I understood that we might have stopped dad's plans, and I remember that I felt ashamed. I thought that maybe we could try again if I learned some English. So I started to study. I had a box in my room, a green box, in which I collected words. I looked up words in a dictionary, wrote them down, and I guessed how to pronounce them.

I sometimes wonder if dad was bitter for us holding him back. If he had applied for citizenship without us, he might have been accepted.

I want to establish: I have mentioned earlier in this book how serious it is to blame children for things they can't help or influence. Dad hadn't put in any kind of effort in teaching us English since he didn't pay attention to us. And my brother, how could he?

The feeling of helplessness and shame from being worthless and without having a chance was devastating. I always tried, though, to influence situations. That's why I collected words in my little green box. Then maybe dad would become happier with us. My lack of self-esteem, of course, has its origin partly in these kinds of events, and I took on the responsibility that wasn't for me to take.

The worst situation of this kind is that I, from the beginning of life, wasn't wanted. My parents already had a girl. Now they wanted a boy. Dad wished a boy so bad, to make him happy, and people around my parents had been telling them for nine months that *"this time it will be a boy."* A boy. A boy.

But I wasn't a boy, so for the first days of my life, I wasn't welcome. Of course, it was very important to my mum to *"give her man a boy, just as he wanted."*

However, everything was better three years later, when they finally had their boy. I have been told that dad jumped up and down in the delivery room, happily exclaiming, *"He has a penis! It's a boy! It's a boy!"*

Please remember to NEVER blame a child for things he or she can't help or influence. Please, please remember that always.

Make Sure Your Children Are Nice to Each Other

I tell: Recently I was at a hotel weekend with my family. That is my husband and children. I don't know why it came over me this morning, but at breakfast the second day, holding my sandwich in my hand, I suddenly exclaimed:

- I'm gonna hold my sandwich like this!

My husband and my children stopped eating and just stared at me.

- What do you mean? my husband asked.

- I said I'm gonna hold my sandwich like this.

As I wrote earlier bullying was going on at home. One of my siblings constantly seemed to look for flaws in me. If there were no flaws to be found at the moment, flaws needed to be found. Among hundreds or maybe a thousand of things that were wrong with me, it was also about how I held my sandwich. I held my sandwich between my ringfinger and my thumb, which means two fingers up. This was apparently one more disturbing thing in the line regarding me. And one more opportunity to tell me that I was a "freak." For many years, and every time I've been eating sandwich during all these years (imagine thirty years of sandwiches) I've been telling myself that it is wrong to hold a sandwich with two fingers up. It has to be only one finger up, "otherwise I'm a freak, and maybe I am…" This has been really, really hard on me. Especially as it has been about my whole person, everything about me – wrong, wrong, wrong.

This morning at the hotel, something important happened within me. I realised that there is nothing wrong holding a sandwich like I did as a child. It was just something that one of my siblings made up to diminish me once again. Me myself would never had noticed such a detail at all to diminish another person. Not in a million years. But it got stuck inside me – the feeling of "wrongness."

I want to establish: Parents have to pay attention to their children's behaviour toward each other. I don't know who caused me most pain and psychological damage - my sibling or my dad.

Diminished for a long time means you may become too weak to think clearly – you buy the fact that you are "wrong" in every way, and you lose your self-confidence.

So, try to see things clearly and hold your sandwich as you wish! Draw a line between what things that really are important to change about yourself and what stuff that is just invented by people who probably are feeling worse than you regarding themselves, and therefore have a need for diminishing you. People are sometimes making things up just to find reasons to bully others. Also siblings sometimes. It's just empty talk. Stay alert as a parent and do not allow your children to destroy each other.

I can't lie. This is an area which is hard to process. To change a self-image where you are totally crushed, it's work around the clock. However, when you have changed the image of yourself, and probably realised that everything has been a lie, you will be able to reach a strong sense of freedom.

Now, back to dad.

Success, Money and Happiness

I tell: Dad dreamed of success. He wanted to invest. He wanted to expand. He wanted to get rich. Probably he would have succeeded if he hadn't lacked social competence and therefore made more enemies than friends.

I experienced dad as an intelligent man when I was a little girl, which doesn't say much. He was simply the best in everything at that time. However, I experienced him as an intelligent man also with my adult, more clear-sighted eyes. IQ wasn't the problem. EQ (Emotional Quotient), emotional intelligence was the real problem. EQ, and also being objective is very important if you should be able to succeed in an arena where there are many other people to collaborate with, that is, an arena like the labour market.

I have always seen my father as a man who believed that money would make him happier. He wanted to spend money, but the result was that he always ended up spending more money than he had.

I want to establish: Achieving dreams and goals in life is important to people; it's a part of our happiness as human beings. But then we also have the unfortunate and distorted belief that money equals happy life. After winning a big amount of money, people become happier – for three months, according to research, but then they are back to the same levels of happiness as before winning the amount. The notion that economic wealth equals happiness was my dad's belief too. Unfortunately, he was looking for happiness in the wrong place.

I belong to the group of people who don't dream of big profits and financial independence. I believe that I will be happier going to my meaningful job every day and knowing that my salary comes from actually having done a job. I also believe that in the long run, I get happier from buying something I have longed for than what I get when I, with millions in my pocket, can buy anything whenever I want it. That is also an attitude and spirit I want to bless my children with. Otherwise, while they are dreaming of great economic wealth, life passes them by because they spend their time thinking about everything they want but not will be able to receive?

Who knows, my children might win a big amount of money or start a very successful business. However, it is not something they should set their mind on to accomplish a happy life, because then I know they are looking for happiness in the wrong place. On the other hand, I also hope they won't be having financial problems from a low wage, and they wouldn't have to live with worries day and night for not being able to pay their bills.

Greed and people's search for glory are destroying the world. Unfortunately, that has been going on way too long already.

Deserve Your Children's Love – For Real

I tell: Yes, I guess we loved dad anyway. He was the one who made our lives work. He was the one who paid for the food on the table and that way, helped us survive. That's the way he wanted us to see him, and he succeeded. He was so important that we loved him.

If we imagine a long, sandy beach with lots, and again lots of sand grains, we were satisfied with one single grain of sand of attention or "love" to compensate for his lack of… well, most things which had to do with the family. We were so starved for attention, love and warmth that the smallest sign of him doing something positive for us made us adore him. I remember once when I had a minor accident with the moped. I got a scratch-wound on one of my arms, and dad put a patch on it. I often think about that now. It seemed like he had a heart in there, though, when it came to him and his interests, it laid deeply embedded.

As an adult, it is heart-breaking that my dad had helped me with some things in my house. He was a carpenter, and some of the changes we made in our house caught his interest. In those instances, he was present and engaged. The traces of him in my house sometimes make me forgive him for everything. I am willing to forgive him for my loveless childhood. These traces have left me in doubt, *"Well, he was a good dad anyway,"* and he was sometimes. But I guess no matter what you achieve as a parent only because of your own interests, only when *you* feel like it, it can't possibly compensate for the fact that you as a parent don't exist in your children's life when they really need you. That is, even if you yourself are in the middle of something. Dad was definitely not there. If he didn't find any interest in a situation himself, he would not be a part of it. Nor was it interesting for him to spend Christmas with us or to show up on our birthdays when we had grown up.

If you didn't agree with him in detail within a project, it became a problem. Then you had to feel stupid as if you didn't understand something common sense, and you also got a bad conscience because you strongly disliked the feeling of not giving dad your support. On a more or less conscious level, we all knew all too well that he needed it. People's support. People's approval. People's interest in him and his ideas. He wanted to reach through with his thoughts, visions and plans. Once again, I felt that even if it was about us, it was still only about him. He left me in a strange feeling of not being worthy of any help. Actually, I don't think that he saw it that way, but I understand that the feeling of having no value as a child has followed me into adulthood in situations like this. So, when he made an effort, I just felt guilty and uncomfortable. I offered to pay him. He declined. And I felt lousy.

I want to establish: In the long run, you can't get away so easily if you want children who don't crash in adolescence, like me. You should not want to get away so easily either, only being there when you feel like it. If we don't want to be together with our children and give them all the warmth we can, we need to start wondering why. I don't want to be adored by my children for starving them on love.

The feeling I have regarding my house may be a part of the dilemma that makes it so difficult you just want to cry. He was kind. He wasn't there for us, but he was kind … I got a grain of sand here, and I got a grain of sand there. This is an extremely unnatural and harmful parent-child relationship. The inner feeling of psychological poisoning is a feeling that cannot be put into words. There is no consolation to be found in this. Not for me. But it comforts me that my children don't understand and nor ever will understand what I'm talking about.

Do Not Make Your Children Feel Sorry for You

I tell: Dad was clearly an expert on keeping us in his grip. He constantly gave us a dose of *"Feel sorry for me-preparation."* It was mainly about his back. He laid on the floor to stretch it out almost every evening, and he complained very much when he was about to get up. We all helped him.

My sister sometimes said: *"Daddy will probably die young. He won't get older than thirty with all that pain and all his hard work."* I was so young and naïve that I believed that she might be right. Of course, it brought fear. Fear from the fact that dad could actually disappear any minute. It was he who kept us alive. It was he who was the important one, and now he was so worn out that he could die.

But one day, as I was walking up the stairs, I saw between steps that he inside the living room stood up completely without a problem. A very first natural thought that struck me was that dad might sometimes be exaggerating, but I never said anything.

I want to establish: After the psychological terror that this was to me as a child – to believe that our important father will not be living so long, I am *extremely* careful in that my children should *never* feel sorry for me. I can sometimes tell them things, they have not completely missed the fact that something has been wrong in my childhood family, but I always say afterwards that I am strong today and that I have learned a lot along the way. That I have made lemonade out of the lemons I received in life, which is the truth.

Acknowledge Your Faults and Shortcomings

I tell: On one occasion, we rented an apartment for a week together with dad's co-worker and his wife. It was a combined business and leisure trip. We also went to the amusement park. Dad showered, and afterwards, when I went to the shower, I discovered that there was only conditioner in the bathroom, no shampoo. I told dad that he probably had washed his hair with conditioner. He silenced me. He did not want his friends to know. Even this was too embarrassing a mistake for him to admit.

I want to establish: Imagine how hard dad must have struggled through life to seem infallible. Even a trivial "conditioner-mistake" in the shower was too embarrassing for him.

The person I myself have become, I have now learned to laugh at my own mistakes. I can tell others about them so that they can have the chance to laugh a little too unless it is a mistake which got serious consequences, of course. In those cases, I instead seek support from others to get help processing my mistake.

When you are not able to admit mistakes and shortcomings and that way show your children that you are a perfect human being, oh, oh, oh – then there is a risk that it will turn out very wrong. Your children should not have any expectations of being perfect. Nor they should believe that you are perfect. We are human beings and should also be allowed to be human beings. I consider this to be a very important building block in establishing self-esteem within our children.

Don't Always Be the "Best"

I tell: I often considered dad as a person who so badly wanted to be the best. He wanted to beat others. He needed it. If someone told him that they had been on the moon, dad had been on Jupiter. *"That was nothing, listen to this…"* He often told people how much he had been through, and sure, he was an adventurous man, a person who wasn't afraid to go into the woods even though he knew there were bears nearby, but it was also important to him to boost about that.

I want to establish: I pity dad because of this and many other things. He didn't know what he had been cheated on. He knew that something was missing, I refer to his last note on his kitchen table, but he never understood what it was or to what extent. My feeling is that he had been deprived of life.

The phenomenon "wanting to be the best" is not only about narcissistic people. I could gabble several names of people, who in my eyes, are completely healthy, but who are driven by a convulsive desire to be the best regarding most areas in life. But consider this:

I may know that I have won a bigger win, went on a bigger rollercoaster or had a more difficult experience. But I still don't need to steal another human beings moment and put myself in the centre. I'm willing to give my friend this moment. It's worth something. There's nothing good about leaving the room with the feeling that I knocked someone down… I don't find any pleasure in doing that. People won't get close to me if I act that way all the time. If it is important to me to tell about myself, I can choose another moment to do so. If I have strong self-esteem, then I will find something else in life other than competing to be the best. I have found peace within myself and am able to enjoy life without constant comparisons. It is a wonderful life. Dad never got the chance to experience that feeling.

Though, it becomes completely unnatural to be a part of a football team and never be interested in winning. Competition is competition. Be a good winner, but also a good loser. When you go home after a match with your child, there should be a break from the feeling of competition for a while. The training between matches is mostly for children to have fun. A life in constant competition does not boost your self-esteem or self-confidence. Self-confidence may be, in case you happen to be very skilled. In future professional life, they should also perform the best they can because they find pleasure or greater meaning in what they do, not to beat everyone around.

Security

I tell: I always was a little bit scared of dad, or at least I held an unhealthy respect for him. A lot in our lives was all about doing a good job. If we did a job together at home, we had our breath in our throats and our hearts constantly beating too fast. If we didn't understand in exactly the same second what he meant we should do and how to act, we were to hear his irritation and sharp words about us being stupid.

I remember a time when boat trips were dad's great interest. As we approached a lock, my panic also approached. The rest of the family had a task. One held a rope in the bow. One held a rope in the stern… I had no assigned task. I was scared because if I happened to be in the way when dad came hurrying in the boat, so he could push, squeeze hard or pinch me. In my home, there was also the old-fashioned misconception that beatings sometimes were an okay method to lead children in the right direction when you found them troublesome. In any case, I took on the only task I could think of in that boat – to concentrate on staying out of the way. Out of *his* way. I mostly succeeded with that task, but I felt so useless, so very, very useless. That he would tuck us in in the evenings and read us a bedtime story, give us a sense of safety in a parental warm way, would probably have been very foreign to us.

Further on the topic of security, or rather insecurity: Sympathising with dad's opinions was almost like riding a roller coaster. As a family member, it was important to think the same way he did. That also applied to mom. While growing up, I have never heard my mother say: *"I think..., I believe..., I want..."* Instead, it was always: *"Dad thinks, dad believes, dad wants..."* Often, to make dad happy, we said things that we knew he would like to hear. It was very important to us to maintain his contentment, to please him and fulfil his wishes. I think that we really wanted to keep him satisfied. I guess that's important to all children; they want their parents to be happy.

Also, when dad wasn't present, I always thought about what he would have thought – what he would have liked and disliked. Perhaps this phenomenon is something positive if the children have healthy parents. Children need their parents' values as support at the beginning of life. But dad wasn't healthy. At first, his opinion may have been that something was incredibly good. Probably it was when things went his way or when he needed someone or something.

However, there were times when his weak self-confidence shown through.

Or, it was when something was interesting or exciting to him that he was in a good mood. It felt good inside when dad was in a good mood upon seeing things positively. It made me happy. When he then changed his mind, we tried to catch on. A person that was raised to the skies one month could next month be an asshole. When I think back, I can still today feel the strain. At first, you're ought to think like this, and then you're ought to think like that. Dad was always right.

I want to establish: Without the feeling of security: No self-esteem. Without self-esteem: No feeling of security. Since I became a parent, I've been looking back at dad as a parent, and then I go in the opposite direction from him in my parental journey. Security is absolutely at the top of my list. Without security, there is nothing to build on. Everything you can possibly think of that may scare your children, stop it. Sometimes children get scared anyway. Try then to talk about it and try to obtain a clear picture of where the feeling of insecurity comes from. Emphasise to your child that you yourself aren't worried. If you are worried and can't hide it, talk about it in such a suitable manner as possible. Let the child talk. Hug your child and show him or her that you are there. No child will grow up to be a mentally healthier person by having experienced fear and insecurity while growing up.

Dad had a fierce temper showing up once and a while. Of course, it's okay to get angry sometimes as a parent when patience runs out. It was, however, never us who made it overflow. We were really too unobtrusive to provoke any outbursts. But when something goes wrong, most of us may lose our temper. When dad lost his temper, we were the ones to blame or get pushed if we happened to stand in his way. This is never okay. I guess we would have felt safer if we had felt a bond with dad, a close and loving bond—an account of trust between parent and child. If we had also talked about anger, just like sometimes the last straw breaks the camel's back, and tried to diffuse the anger or reduce it by a burst of redemptive laughter, maybe we could have handled it better. In dad's case, the feeling of insecurity totally took over when the mood swung. Pinching, squeezing, pushing, insulting or giving punishment as part of parenting strategies is immensely wrong and very harmful. As a parent, you must immediately apply for help if you are doing this to your child. You need to apply for both; therapy for yourself and acquiring the right parental education that involves learning appropriate strategies for raising children.

The fact that dad changed his mind all the time also led to the feeling of insecurity. At the beginning of life, children often create their values with help from parents as a part of their social heritage.

Children who have destructive parents with skewed values and have the presence of mind and strength to protest may be treated badly in their homes. As a consequence of this treatment, they may feel so broken inside that outwardly, they are seen as troublemakers by everyone. It is depressing that these children may actually be the ones with the best understanding and the clearest interpretation of the situation of us all but are punished because of it.

The values that I create as a child are, in fact, part of who I am becoming. At home, there was no stable base to stand on. No peace was around to be able to create these values. Nothing ever ended well. I was disappointed again and again. However, I wasn't disappointed with dad. No, he was the proper one and the one always being right. Instead, I got disappointed with the outside world and the people in it. My perception ended up in the fact that the world around us was probably quite a dark place because there was so much in it, which turned out to be bad in the end. Always bad in the end. And this was the world that I myself would be facing in time… an unfair, unpredictable and insecure world.

Fortunately, it turned out that everything and everyone wasn't so hopeless after all. Unfortunately, till realising that, I was no longer a child.

Dad experienced himself being a victim of external circumstances. He was a victim, yes, but not in the way he himself believed. He constantly believed that it was all the other people who were "wrong," and sure, sometimes you do meet, and excuse me for this - real dummies. In dad's perspective, though, he was the victim because he was unable to handle the social life. He lacked acceptance. He lacked in so many areas, and this was a consequence of his childhood.

Respect

I tell: We had a midsummer party. A few days before, I had been to the bank opening my first bank account at the age of thirteen years old. My sister was there too. I was nervous when I walked towards the counter, and I asked my sister what I should say. She replied: *"Say: I want to open a bank account which I can deposit money and withdraw* *money."* This statement from my sister conveyed that there are bank accounts in which you can deposit money but not withdraw to get better interest rates.

This became a funny story to tell at the midsummer party, the way I had made a fool of myself. *Why on earth should one have a bank account if not to deposit and withdraw money?!* I was mocked in front of all the guests who laughed out loud at dad's narration of the story as I sat there ashamed. My sister did not want to say anything about this statement being her idea. Otherwise, she would be laughed at too.

I want to establish: Before you tell others about your child, think very carefully. People laughing at you, yes, adults might have found things I said very cute, but I said it from a lack of experience, and not to sound funny or entertain my parents' friends. As a child I implemented these experiences in my mind as a truth sounding like this: *"Make mistakes equals not loved."*

Be Interested in Your Grown-up Child

I tell: Dad's interest for me did not exist in adulthood either. I chose boyfriends that didn't get dad's approval, and I suffered very badly from that. I chose a career that did not interest him. When I chose college education, he doubted my choice: *"The Children and Leisure Program."* The word leisure, well, he was allergic to it. That word could mean that people were lazy. He didn't understand that the program was all about working with children and young people.

When I was about to graduate as a teacher in my early twenties, it would have felt good to have a dad asking how my studies were going, how I experienced the demanding final exam, if I had been looking for a job, and in that case where. Not one single question came from his end. Not when I started my first job as a teacher either. I probably would have gotten more interest from dad if I had chosen a career that interested him. If I had become a craftswoman, I'm sure he would have been interested. Then, however, I would have been given the disadvantage of listening to him telling me that I was an idiot, not understanding anything. That is if we would have been working together, which in the latter case would have been expected from me. If not working with him, I would have felt his disappointment within me for the rest of my life.

The strange thing is, dad wanted to study further as a young man. I have been asking myself if that is the explanation to why dad didn't support me. Was he jealous?

I sometimes got that feeling. But I think jealousy is just what it seemed to be. In fact, I think that he was afraid of me running him over. I became a potential threat to his extremely fragile self-image. I refer to the beginning of this book where I wrote about the origins of narcissism within a person.

I remember an occasion on my birthday. I was an adult, but DESPITE EVERYTHING, I thought it would be nice to invite him to a birthday party. Dad replied: *"Well, if it's a rainy day, I can come, but if it's sunny weather, I would rather go to the caravan and barbecue."* Dad also had a period when the caravan was his great interest, after the hunting and the music.

On my next birthday, I didn't invite to any party. Mom came to us for an hour or so and congratulated me. Dad was on the job fifty miles away and lived during this work trip in the caravan. When mom was at our place, he called her and asked where she was. She told him that she was with me. Hopeful and a bit curious, I wondered if he at least would say hello and congratulate me over the phone, but no. He just wondered when mom would bring the food.

After that, I never had a birthday party. He burned all hope I'd ever had from a father figure.

I want to establish: With the powerful appearance of a narcissistic parent, the parent's opinion becomes so *incredibly* important to the child. It is to me sometimes unbearable to think about the fact that my opinion regarding myself for a very long time was entirely based on my dad's, my sibling and other people's pictures of me. That means no clear picture at all. The picture that still existed was extremely negative, built on others empty talk. No wonder I had so many problems within myself when my self-image, which one cannot even say existed at all, was crushed.

Children need their parents even as adults. If parents behave like "take the opportunity" to run off and disappear when their children have grown up, it just shows once more that something is terribly wrong. To the child, it is confirmed again that he or she is an absolute nobody. Over and over again. An emptiness takes place in the heart of the child as a consequence of parental absence. Children are doomed to struggle with this emptiness their whole lives. They are doomed to try to fill it with the most easing thoughts or activities they can think of. At this point, it goes wrong for many young people. They do not succeed in saving themselves.

A difficult dilemma, which has taken a lot of happiness and energy, is the fact that dad never acted, keeping in mind my family's situation at the moment, that is me, my husband and my two children. He completely lacked the ability to put himself into our position, starting from what we were doing at the moment or what we wanted, what we were thinking or what we believed. He always proceeded from his point of view and expected us to fit into his plans and his will.

My last text message from dad was about moose meat. During my pregnancies, I was sensitive to tastes, like many other mothers to be. Moose meat did not taste well. After that, I started to decline when dad wanted to bring moose meat. He couldn't accept this. Therefore, my last text message from dad was of the aggressive kind, filled with contempt regarding my ruthless behaviour towards him. If we didn't adapt, we had to listen to his disappointment, his irritation over us being ungrateful. Then I, of course, felt lousy. Again.

Over time, after becoming a mother, I chose to avoid contact with dad. I want my children to embrace an image of reciprocity and interest between people. I also want them to gain some kind of understanding when it comes to his disorder. I want them to know that he had his lacking personality for a reason. Many people are narcissistic, and there are often explanations to find back in time.

A child who has grown up with a narcissistic parent is waiting to be seen. It takes time to realise that the confirmation regarding them being loved the way they wish for will never come. It takes time to realise that they never will be seen for their choices and for the people that they are. The emptiness that they are feeling from not being seen will be poisoning. The best way to detox themselves and heal is to cut the ribbons, ribbons that do not even exist. Only when they succeed to embrace the fact and start to build themselves out of their own strength can they be free. There will probably be a psychological crash before they are able to start climbing uphill with their own power, but with the support from growing self-esteem, it is possible. It is a long and difficult road to walk, but it's probably the only way to get to live a free and happy life as an adult. A piece of advice is to start studying how to create self-esteem and then maintain it.

The emptiness I experienced very strongly before my crash a number of years ago, the emptiness I've carried inside my whole life, caused me a lot of stress. A life without self-esteem may be a stressful life because you are searching for confirmation that you are good enough and through this, keep your nose above the water surface. Suicide plans are probably not at all uncommon in this state. To me, a life with self-esteem means inner peace. I never have to be the best at anything at all. I don't need to win any discussions, well, unless it is a discussion of crucial importance regarding any of my children or a student of mine. To win a discussion just for winning is insignificant to me, even at times I happen to know I'm right. I never have to compete to receive prestige – because that is not my aim. I'm still an ambitious person, but compared to before, I'm on half speed. Earlier, I really performed way too much every day, and that too under devastating levels of stress. What I achieve today keeps me healthy. Today I am calm and satisfied. It is a wonderful life, and most important; Today, I want to live!

Summary Thoughts

It may be a good idea to think about what kind of self-image we want to send our children out to live with. Are they nobody? Or are they somebody? Do they feel valued? It may also be worth considering what values we want to send with our children. As children they will have a hard time being strong on their own. Think about the type of people you like to surround yourself with. What values do these people hold?

What values do you yourself hold which make you feel good and be able to succeed in relationship with others? It may be valuable to think about how you should behave to send these particular values to your children. We cannot teach valuable lessons to our children by telling them one thing and behaving otherwise – a fact that has been known for quite a while now.

We need to provide our children wings that they can fly into life with. Growing up with a narcissistic parent didn't give me the wings I needed or the wings that would have made me feel good and safe. I have managed to create wings for myself as an adult, but I still don't fly well in certain situations.

Sometimes people get to hear that they almost should be grateful for their upbringing because that is what made them who they are. *But*, nothing can ever compensate for not receiving wings from the start of life. Having a hard time as a child cannot be turned into a positive thing; neither can it be ignored as if it didn't matter. Instead, we make as much juice we can possibly ever make. All the time, we try to use our experiences to something which makes sense. Making sense of things is like patches on our bodies, which is needed because the sorrows remain within us. There are deep wounds. To us, it is very important to keep in mind that when we are flying inside a dark tunnel, we will always come out from the other side. The feeling of hollowness sometimes gets to us. Sometimes I have thought that it's okay that life has been difficult sometimes because every single experience has led to the life I have today, and today I am happy. It is a comforting thought which I sometimes fully accept. But no matter how I look at it, I can never escape from the fact that there is a difference between bad things that happened and the life experiences I got and not having received wings as a child. We must also remember that some children who have not received wings do not only have trouble flying themselves, they also make others crash.

Give your children wings from the start. The children whose parents fail, we need to help them to at least become Dandelion Children. Their wings may not be as large and powerful as the early childhood wings, but if someone helps to save them, then a little later, they will still be able to fly.

In my book *Safe Harbour*, you can read a lot more about building self-esteem, both within yourself and within your children. By the way – there is an important connection to find between the two of them. As a consequence of my childhood, I did have parenting flaws at the beginning of motherhood, which I do not hide in that book. Being honest with yourself is a crucial component required to improve.

Dandelion Children

Heritage and Environment

Something I have thought a lot about is how children, later adults, who mourn their childhood can grow up to be almost like their parents or exact copies of their parents. They may even hate their parents for what they have done, but that won't prevent them from copying them either. As you learn more about personality disorders, then you understand the reasons for such behaviour. A narcissistic person affects his children so strongly through the environment they shared during the child's upbringing that the children are at risk of becoming the same. If they become the same, they do not see it because they, just like their parent, defend themselves with them being infallible.

These children have often not received help in early childhood to get through normal childhood narcissism. They have not received help with parents setting necessary boundaries without shame and guilt – not being forgiven for mistakes, and they have probably not had their needs met in other areas either. On the other hand, they have also been defended by parents in a totally unreasonable manner when they've done something wrong outside their home, to another child or an adult. When you go outside the family, it is rarely the narcissist's child who has done something wrong. In that case, it would cause shame within the parent, and that is forbidden. With such unrealistic support, the child may learn that it is very important to seem infallible, no matter how wrong you have done. When it comes to narcissism, some researchers also talk about a genetic inheritance that is likely to exist. When I hear this, I think of the children who withdraw – "because they are right." If these children grow up raised by a narcissistic parent, how should they be able to turn out right? The inheritance, along with the environment, may bring a child double bad luck in life.

Although I nowadays know why children of narcissistic parents may actually become narcissistic themselves, it feels unbelievable that they can really do the same things, act the same way as the parent did and still not see it. It's like something isn't connecting. Everyone else sees that they move in the same way, talk in the same way, have the same facial expressions, treat other people the same way – some are actually worth something for the moment; others can be treated like dirt. They can be just as arrogant and just as jealous of others, put the blame on others… we can actually continue for a long time. *But the individual in question can't see it!* They really don't see it! For the rest of us, that is as difficult to understand, just like the infinity of the universe or other such totally intangible phenomenon.

When it comes to psychopathic individuals, they may as well as narcissistic individuals have inherited their personality disorder genetically. Though, we must not give up hope there. Instead, we should be aware of the fact that there are well-functioning people around us who have these differences, abnormalities in the brain. Those individuals have most likely grown up in a well-functioning home in a predictable and loving environment. But here, too, children can be affected twice by having inherited parent's flawed genes while also remaining in a home with a psychopathic parent.

The Social Heritage

The Swedish psychiatrist Gustav Jonsson launched during the 60's the concept of social heritage. In a doctoral dissertation, he shows an explanatory model of why children end up in dysfunctional lives in one way or another. The explanation is that the parents' social difficulties are inherited into the children. This environmental explanatory model stands next to the genetic heritage for the issue of heritage or environment, which can be applied to a variety of areas concerning a person's life, health and behaviours.

As we are familiar with since earlier, children sometimes bring their parents habits and behavioural patterns into their own lives as adults. It can also turn out in the opposite way. The children don't become like their parents at all but are still weighed down due to a less favourable environment while growing up. As a child, you don't choose your parents, and we know that the social heritage may have been passed on through generations.

The social heritage is thus behaviours that we inherit. We are influenced by the environment, we adapt to the environment that surrounds us, and accordingly, we behave in a certain way. It is a fact that many of us turn out to be like our parents because we have lived many years together with them. We are socialised into the patterns of behaviour which we have experienced at home. We may also choose the same profession and have the same view of education, a positive view as well as a negative one.

I have experienced that children who come from a less favourable environment sometimes grow up with the feeling of emptiness, being hollow. Every one of them tries to fill it. They are sentenced for life, sentenced to a constant search for what could be wrong. Some of them try to fill this hole inside by using drugs or by criminal behaviour, while others, despite the situation, choose a functional way of life.

So there are children who, despite a certain social heritage, choose their own path in life and eventually become a person different from their parents. It does not have to be in a positive manner, nor negative. However, it is positive in those times when children of parents having, for example, alcohol abuse or a personality disorder and/or violent behaviour, physical or mental violence, choose to go their own way and break a dysfunctional social heritage. This choice may partly have an explanation in the fact that there have been other people around the actual child while growing up, who have made an impression on them and helped them to take a different view of life from their parents'. These children are called Dandelion Children. A Dandelion has the power to grow through asphalt and still become a Dandelion in bloom. A child can grow up in a very destructive environment and still create a stable life as an adult.

Breaking the Social Heritage

Now, let's talk about the children who grew up in homes strongly controlled by a narcissistic or psychopathic parent or with other problems in their family but, despite this, become completely different from them in adulthood. They receive another view of fellow human beings – one based on totally different behavioural patterns, self-chosen professions, and different views on parenting… completely different in all matters. How come that there are children who break the social legacy? How come there are Dandelion Children? How come they turn out being so different from the rest of their family and, yes, maybe also different from a large part of all their relatives? Are there genetic explanations? Is it due to education? Interests? Random meetings? One possible explanation has already been mentioned previously; somebody, maybe someone from outside, has made a strong impression on them. A positive impression.

Sometimes I thank my teenage friends for breaking up my social heritage. When I started high school, I made friends. Many friends. Some of them woke me up. They woke my earliest thoughts about something might be wrong. In their homes, it was different. In other friends' homes, however, it could be at least as difficult as in my home, where my dad ruled, and sibling bullying was going on. One of my friends had a dad who was an alcoholic, and it was very problematic at times. I sometimes think: If it hadn't been for those people who aroused my early thoughts, had I then been the one I am today?

I have always been a relatively social person, despite the circumstances, despite my background and despite the feeling of insecurity that I obtained from these circumstances. In primary and middle school, bullying was so common to children in my class that there was no such thing as getting support from positive references. There was a threatening atmosphere in the class, and it created social insecurity. But from the age of thirteen, I have always been standing with one leg in the narcissistic dysfunctional world and one leg in the healthy, well-functioning world. Being social is a very important protective factor. My friends, together with their families, made a strong impression on me. I there felt that I wasn't "wrong." At home, I was often tormented by the fact that I didn't fit in. I have realised that I was rejected just because of the fact that I was different. At the age of nineteen, I had almost fully revealed the skewed family situation to myself, thanks to the exposure I received.

It wasn't my references that were wrong. I had caught sight of the psychologically healthy, and I kept on walking their way.

Something that I feel extremely happy about is the fact that I was never judged by anyone, even though people knew about my father and grandfather. The people around me saw me for who I was. It proves to me that only we decide who we want to be and how we come across to others. We must not forget that. We must also remember to act the same way that all people surrounding me always have acted – Not judging people because of their origin.

My boyfriend back in the nineties sometimes said that he had never met anyone like my dad. He then didn't mean that he had discovered something positive. He had been exposed to dad's bad behaviour when they worked together. My boyfriend was not primarily my boyfriend in dad's eyes. Instead, he should prove himself to my dad as a well-functioning workforce. However, to dad, there was no man who could prove himself good enough for longer than a few weeks or months.

Coming to my boyfriend's view of my dad, there was a reason that he hadn't met anyone like my father earlier. It's not very common with people like him, after all, and he hadn't run into anyone with narcissistic tendencies before. In my life, though, it has been so common that I feel that I've understood the patterns, the social heritage, explanations back in time, and my own journey into a normal, well-functioning world.

An important survival factor for me has been gratefulness. I have always been extremely grateful for everything that has actually been working well in life. In tough times you have to be grateful for the small things. I also have the ability to make juice out of lemons. I understand that I have always had a sense of gratitude but also a sense of coherence.

SOC – A Sense of Coherence

"SOC refers to knowing that I have the power to constantly influence, constantly be involved in my own life. In other words, it's me who decides, it's me who makes it happen, and I have got the tools for it. Aaron Antonovsky's theory has proved applicable to everything from leadership to personal development, personal responsibility – A more harmonious life." [34]

---

[34] https://aktivt-valmående.se/?p=61

A researcher named Aaron Antonovsky, born in the 1920's is a researcher who has taken a different input and interest in health than most others. He took an interest in the women who had survived the holocaust. Instead of looking into the causes of why they were in poor health, he took the perspective of why some of them were actually in good health.

His research has shown us that twenty-nine per cent of the women experienced they were in good health despite all their horrible experiences. How come they experienced good health? It turned out that these women had a high Sense of Coherence. Antonovsky found out that people who choose to focus on positive factors, the areas which actually are well-functional rather than the negative areas where they are non-functional, stick to better health than others. They build themselves up by focusing on what's good and avoid digging around in what's bad. It sounds incredible that these women could find something positive to set focus on while being locked up in Nazi concentration camps, and of course, there was not. However, they chose the attitude that they would use their experiences in a way that could affect the present and the future. And make sense of it. They found ways to deal with the most horrific occurrence that people may get to experience.

I have myself listened to one of these women (and also a man) who survived the Holocaust. They told us, young people, about their experiences, and they showed us the number on their arms. They wanted to influence the future. I don't think that any of us young people who were there have forgotten about them. They were the primary masters regarding making juice from the sourest lemons humanity has ever experienced.

Through my work as a teacher, I came across the concept of SOC – The Sense of Coherence. During the days of education in this area, I found it had obvious and direct connections to my life even though the Holocaust, of course, is an extremely much more devastating experience. A study carried out at a Swedish university, *"What makes the Dandelions grow,"* confirms my experiences regarding these educational days. SOC is in this report mentioned as one of the most important factors for children to be able to create a functional life as adults, despite an unfavourable upbringing. The SOC has three main components:

Comprehensibility

Structure and regularity in life are important to most people. We want to be able to predict what's going to happen, and if something still surprises us, we want to be able to explain it. People who are good at making events in life comprehensible lead a healthier life [35].

Manageability

When the outside world is demanding, and when unfortunate events occur, it is important that we do not see ourselves as helpless victims. It is important that the person experiences that he or she has the resources to deal with adversity. People who feel they can handle their lives become more resilient to ill-health [36].

Meaningfulness

For us to feel good, it is also important that we meet challenges in which we find worth investing energy. We need to find meaning in what we do. People who also try to

---

[35] https://lattattlara.com/klinisk-psykologi/KASAM/

[36] https://lattattlara.com/klinisk-psykologi/KASAM/

find meaning within unfortunate events that happen in life, as a matter of fact, feel better than those who don't [37].

Children with a high level of SOC do have resilience and are able to recover quickly after stressful situations. Children who early in life succeed in their analysis of situations and are able to reason with themselves may understand a lot over time which is very important, especially if something is wrong at home. This probably leads to an ability to rise again and again and brush off psychological stress. They have a kind of ability to detoxify themselves. Qualities within the children have an enormous significance. These qualities include intelligence, curiosity, accommodating behaviour, humour, problem-solving ability and social skills. These are important protective factors. The children handle their situation by pulling back for the moment, they try to adapt to the situation, and they try to understand. Furthermore, it is important to the children to have, if only, one single adult, to give warmth and love during childhood to be able to function adequately. Both internal and external factors such as surrounding circumstances and the characteristics within

---

[37] https://lattattlara.com/klinisk-psykologi/KASAM/

child itself play a role when it comes to having a favourable upbringing and a good life in adulthood [38]. Being social and having a high level of SOC, are important protective factors for a Dandelion Child.

Not all people are social, but if we could help them raise their Sense of Coherence, maybe then they could grow, feel more secure and dare to open up more to other people.

My Happiness

When I was younger, I often carried a weight on my shoulders. No one has ever succeeded in taking away my joy totally, though. In tough times, I had been afraid of the fact that my light, my spark, would wear out. However, I learned to find my way back to the joy and meaningfulness of life.

Certainly, I have been thinking of myself as a victim for longer periods, for example, when I was a teenager and had an eating disorder and when I was a child being bullied. Still, usually, I quickly managed to find my way back to my own little sparkle of life. Although I didn't realise until now that it has saved me from burning out. Otherwise, I probably

---

[38] Engström, L & F (2012) *Vad får maskrosorna att växa?* Umeå universitet.

would have seen myself as a full-time victim and at risk of developing in the narcissistic direction.

Who can say they are okay? I have managed to create a well-functioning life as an adult, yes. However, I have suffered too. But I guess you can't say that a Dandelion Child is so very positive and optimistic that he or she is not at all influenced by his or her upbringing. Even though I had lots of creativity that helped me rise and shine, and I sooner or later returned to my joy, I have lived most of my life with performance-based self-esteem. I did not receive my wings as a child.

I am now squeezing this family lemon in order to understand better. I have understood why I often have felt so hollow during life. Children of narcissists are at great risk of spending their lives with that feeling because they have grown up as nobody at all. But I also understand why nothing has been completely extinguishing to me. After a while in the land of sadness, I always start reflecting, and I then put it into my bank of experiences, my life puzzle. That way, I handle it better. SOC – it is very important to me to understand what's going on around me. When something bad happens, I nowadays think: *"Okay, what is it that life wants me to learn this time?"*

I'm constantly trying to achieve these three abilities; comprehensibility, manageability and meaningfulness. I've always done it, even though this ability has increased with age. SOC is something to work with all the time. It is not given that the Sense of Coherence and self-esteem stay at a high level if you don't work with them. If I don't understand what's happening around me, I will probably get confused and frustrated. If I don't understand it, then I can't handle it, and the frustration grows even more. I then experience that my life makes no sense, which is a quite obvious consequence if I don't understand my life… How can I feel happy then? The poisoning and stress that we experience while being affected by a personality disordered individual can be due to a struggle between a healthy person's SOC and the chaos created by the disordered one. This kind of behaviour will rule out our understanding and our manageability in life. A healthy brain isn't shaped to foresee the next step.

The levels of SOC can also vary depending on where you are and depending on what you do. In completely new situations, you will probably have low levels of SOC. It just helps to keep on striving for a little while until it feels better. Those people who usually have high levels of Sense of

Coherence do not in those new situations consider themselves to be victims. Instead, they see themselves in a situation where they have a chance to learn new things. They usually succeed because they immediately get on with their task, and from that, they create their Sense of Coherence. For me, it is highly meaningful to be able to help others by sharing my experiences. Finding meaning in unfortunate events, which is a part of Antonovsky's theory, is the reason why I now am writing this book. To make a sentence of my existence, I must strive towards understanding, putting matters in context. I feel much better if I try to understand why people do what they do instead of just being angry with them. For me, it's therapy. However, that does not mean that I forgive everyone for everything all the time, but I *create an understanding of their behaviour.*

Have you ever experienced that things happen for a reason? *"It feels like this was meant to happen...,"* *"It feels like it was meant for me to meet this person today."* As if it just comes over us… It is *ourselves* who create meaning and significance from our events and meetings. *We* create a sentence, and we are grateful to achieve comprehensibility. Our insight and understanding make life manageable for us. Be proud next time you think that something happened for a reason. It is that you have the ability to create a sense of coherence in your life that comes to light.

Some Are Lucky, Others Not

Children who grow up in safe homes are likely to automatically receive help in reaching a high level of SOC, as they have parents who assist with a sense of meaning, talk to their children and explain what is happening around them. Of course, they support the children in dealing with conflicts and other things that arise in their lives, so they don't find themselves helpless in trying situations. Children need to know that they have the opportunity to influence and to be involved in their own lives. They need to feel that they have got the tools to make things happen. It will give them a more harmonious life now and in their future.

During a parental meeting, the three concepts of comprehensibility, manageability and meaningfulness were discussed. The parents were asked to think for a moment about how to help their children to create a Sense of Coherence. The following are their responses:

Comprehensibility

- Show and explain

- Discuss

- Communicate

- Seek information

- Show them in practice if you are able to

- Give examples

- Give time

- Listen to what they have to say

- Ask further what they think

- Ask open-ended questions

Manageability

- Let them know that they can always talk to us

- Get peppering

- Set a good example regarding how we handle cases

- Help them to feel safe enough to dare

- Work for a good self-esteem

- Help manage social codes

- Make them aware that everyone is different and that there are explanations for it.

- If we can respond to the children's feelings with calmness (Low Arousal Approach), then it can be reflected in the children.

Meaningfulness

- To help them see a context regarding home and school.

- Listen

- Spend time together, have fun

- Help children to feel that they are competent

- Praise

Feel free to continue filling out these lists on your own.

Not everyone is lucky enough to receive this help in their family or has these abilities within themselves as "innate." My dad was born in the 1950's, probably without favourable genetic traits in his personality to create a Sense of Coherence on his own. This was a long time ago, and at that time, students were also just students, not children from a modern school point of view. The children in our society were at the time definitely not *everyone's children.*

What if I had a time machine and was able to go back to the 50's and help my poor dad to understand what happened, what it was due to, that it was wrong and not healthy, and told him what I know today in as much appropriate a way as possible. Stay for a while and then be able to return once and a while. Be that person. Dad never received help or opportunity to grow as a person – for real. Children of a dysfunctional parent often live in an unpredictable world. There is no logic. One matter may not at all have any connections to the other matter, but it is still argued in favour of what the parent wants. Suddenly things just happen without explanations, and I'm not referring to exciting surprises. Instead, I refer to things that the adults suddenly come up with, things they want to do. This is a world without logic and a totally unpredictable existence for a child. In all this, far from all children are able to create a Sense of Coherence, which is so very important to their health and future.

There are children who have high levels of SOC in school, where most things happen in a predictable manner, but at home, they get their legs swept away. That's why daycare and school are incredibly important places for many children. These institutions are not just important to help children with their Sense of Coherence, but also because there are educated staff who may be able to see through the children's situation and detect the children who don't want their holidays. If the parents are dysfunctional, and we now have become aware, we may be able to help those children and young people who, perhaps unknowingly, miss all the important components in their lives. We need to help children manage their lives in the beginning so that they themselves eventually gain a sense of security in knowing that it is possible to steer their own lives, and they decide where life takes them. We need to contribute a sense of meaning to their lives.

An increasing number of young people seem to fall into depression. They lose joy, laughter and a sense of meaning. I want to influence my children with the knowledge that small things in life can be very valuable. I want to send them out to live with great gratitude for the positive things that happen around them. It's a good thing when schools are working with the concept of SOC. We will create the best environment for all of our children if both home and schools know about Aaron Antonovsky and his thoughts and strive to implement them into reality.

Comprehensibility in Time

The healthiest view, in the long run, is perhaps, even if it hurts, to receive help seeing and understanding that something is wrong if you grow up in an unfavourable environment and for a long time believe that everything is the way it should be... well, so it was to me. I saved myself later, but oh, what it had cost me of life until then! When I had my children, I decided that their upbringing would be different. Here comes number five again: *"If none of these 'protective barriers' work, then only the children can save themselves. It is far from all children who succeed."* One of the "telephone-dad's" children will probably become a Dandelion Child. She will be able to grow through the asphalt. The girl who talked to her father on the phone that day had discovered her father's psychopathic personality, and she started to question. Once this disorder catches her eyes, she will continue to see it because her dad will show her the negative sides of himself more and more often the more she questions him. He defends himself, and to her, the truth will become increasingly clear. She is taking a healthy person's perspective without co-dependency, and then it becomes obvious. If her father now goes in one direction, she will probably go in the opposite direction. Maybe she is moving as far away as possible as an adult. Hopefully, she succeeds in breaking the social legacy and protect her future children from the same.

In this family, though, there were more children. The phone girl had several siblings. There were children who didn't question their father. Children who may resemble him in the future, inspired by his strong appearance and personality. Security is a concept which really doesn't belong here, but sometimes this strong appearance within a narcissistic or psychopathic person can be perceived as security by the child; *Dad has the strength and ability to protect me from other people if needed, and that may be necessary.* The children can never be expected to understand from the beginning that it is, in fact, the father that they need to protect themselves from. A psychopathic parent is unable to help the children create a Sense of Coherence because everything is about the parent's life and coherence, or rather lack of it.

We know that structure and regularity are important for comprehensibility. Structure and regularity are probably nothing that a person suffering from a personality disorder can offer.

Also Dandelions Suffer

We must not forget that even if the children succeed in creating a functioning life as adults, they hold an infinite amount of sorrows in their hearts. Anything else is hardly possible for an emotionally healthy person. I'm a Dandelion child. My dad was narcissistic, but I'm writing books about children and self-esteem. I work every day to help children grow. To become independent in thought. Find happiness and joy as a springboard to life. That is my wish. I always try to make juice out of my lemons. Dad died with the lemons in his hand. It hurts my heart to think about that.

I have my writing to thank for a lot in life. Due to the poison that existed within dad, no one in the family could grow. He did not have the time or personality to help someone else grow. Instead, he invested in himself. None of the rest of us got the chance to become someone. My writing of *"Safe Harbour"* was like therapy, helping me to become someone, after all the years, as nobody at all. It is a difficult life to live as nobody at all. The problems pile up one by one, and you sometimes have a hard time seeing an end to it. You do not always see what the solutions would be. You don't even know what's wrong, really.

A little scary, but it has now dawned on me that I too have carried one or two narcissistic qualities within myself, namely the performance-based self-esteem and the feeling of emptiness. I, just like my father, have been poisoned by a narcissistic heritage. If I had not been a part of coherence in general life, for example, at school and with friends, I might have become narcissistic myself. I grew up in an environment where I didn't count. In case something was to be seen, it was an achievement. I have been stuck in stress for a long time over performing as much as possible in an as short time as possible. If I didn't perform, I felt empty.

When I was young, I studied very hard. I sat down doing my homework for hours and hours after school every day. In the evening, before dad arrived from work, sometimes I'd sit down in the armchair to watch something on the TV before going to bed. But when I heard dad's footsteps outside, I'd literally jump out of the armchair, turn the TV off and put my hands into work. If not, I would be putting myself at the risk of being reprimanded for being a lazy person, and being lazy was the ugliest, ugliest you could be in our whole world.

After me breaking contact with my family for a long period of time, to be neutral to myself during a renovation of my body and soul (instead of my house), I built up incipient

258

self-esteem. A self-esteem that I should have received already as a child.

I have now completely obliterated the feat of achievement within myself and filled my gaping hollowness with a wonderful sense of life – self-esteem. Today I perform in moderation, and I do it because it feels good within my heart, because it brings meaning into my life. This feeling is what I want to pass on to my children and my students. In my earlier books, I didn't tell that I grew up with a narcissistic father, nor did I know the concept at the time. And it wouldn't have been good to write about it at the time. Not good at all. At least so I thought. I don't think that dad ever took the time to read my books, so it probably wouldn't have mattered if I did write about it. It struck me, though, that perhaps he should have read them.

Disappearing is exactly what may happen to a child growing up with a narcissistic parent without becoming like him or her. In my case, I disappeared. I was also bullied at school and at home as a consequence of not being anyone. I was an incredibly easy target and prey. *"The uncertainty and the difficulties of asserting makes children easily defeated* victims. *Others continue to take advantage of them as they are accustomed* to." [39]

Still, I have always found my way back to my own little happiness. I found something that I found meaningful. I saw the possibilities just inside the walls of my room. I would, let's say, get the hold of a shoebox, and I made something out of it. Things that many children would have thought were meaningless and banal at the same age, but I saw meaning in them. I had my creativity.

My family could not have been discovered by society. I have thought about that several times. Schools weren't able to identify–us even if they scanned carefully; the bullying, yes, the home situation, no. As for myself, I was an extremely kind and well-behaved child.

Unfortunately, being well-behaved is not always the same thing as being a complete and happy person. Though, without knowledge and solid experience, they would never have detected my situation. It was not discovered by my mother either. My mother was far too controlled by my father. His words were her law. She admired her husband

---

[39] Hotchkiss, S (2008) *Why is it always about you?* The Free Press.

immensely. As I mentioned earlier, she never said what she thought about anything. She talked *through* dad, rattled his opinions on all possible issues. Like Julia Roberts in *Run Away Bride*, who chose to have her eggs served as her husband wanted them, mum wanted the same as dad in life. Mom didn't exist within herself either. There was nothing wrong with dad, though. No, no, no. If there was anyone who was wrong, it was she, herself. Dad was right. In everything. Still, she provided some kind of security, which to some extent compensated for dad's lack of abilities to be a father. Unfortunately, she wasn't emotionally available to the extent that is needed from a mother. That's how I experienced it.

The Attachment Theory

As we have learned, it is important that at least one healthy and loving person is present in a future Dandelion child's life. An adult who is able to provide a sense of security and predictability early in life. In my particular case, grandmother was a very caring person. Of course, we want all children to have a good life from the beginning. If that doesn't work, we want them to at least become Dandelion Children, the next best situation for a child. It's far from certain that the adult security-giving person is to be found within the family or in the immediate surroundings. A pre-school teacher can turn into a very significant adult for a little one. I hope that most people working with our youngest children thrive in their workplaces so that as many changes as possible could be avoided in these environments.

The attachment theory (J. Bowlby) must share some space here. It represents the basis for a child's sense of security. In that regard, four different attachment patterns have been identified:

- A secure attachment pattern – Secure attachment occurs when the infant or child is cared for by available, sensitive and responsive caregivers who are accepting and cooperative, promoting trust and competence. These children, therefore, trust their parent (or the one who mainly takes care of him or her). The caregiver is always there to help the child through difficult or frightening situations.

As adults, it is easy for them to get close to other people, but they are also fine with spending time by their selves. They function well in long term-relationships [40].

---

[40]https://www.psykologiguiden.se/rad-och-fakta/relationer/anknytning/
https://sites.uea.ac.uk/providingasecurebase/attachment-patterns

- An insecure and avoidant attachment pattern – When the caregiver finds it difficult to accept or respond sensitively to the infant's needs, the infant may find that their demands are rejected, their feelings minimised and that the caregiver tries to take over in an intrusive, insensitive way. The child learns to shut down his or her feelings in order to avoid upsetting the caregiver. They are expecting themselves to be rejected when they need help. Therefore, they learn to not seek closeness and support. Instead, they will try and manage their lives on their own. Eventually, they shut down feelings, and instead of using feelings as a compass, they try to *think* to find answers.

As adults, they are often liked by people around them, and they work well in superficial relationships. In close relationships, they keep their distance. It may be difficult to get close to them, especially if they experience expectations of closeness.

- An insecure and ambivalent attachment pattern – In contrast, where the caregiver responds to the infant's demands, but only in a sporadic, unpredictable and at times insensitive fashion, the infant finds it difficult to achieve proximity in a reliable way. Care and protection are sometimes available, but caregiving is uncertain and ineffective. These children carry within their memories experiences of sometimes being cared for and sometimes rejected when seeking help and comfort. The uncertainty makes them feel anxiety regarding separations and also fear. They are often driven by their emotions. As adults, they may be perceived as creative people who are close to their emotions. In close relationships, they often scare people away by their strong desire for closeness. Some of them are so afraid of being abandoned that they instead avoid close relationships altogether.

- An insecure and disoriented attachment pattern – This attachment pattern occurs when the caregiver is rejecting, unpredictable, and frightening or frightened, while the infant is caught in a dilemma of 'fear without solution.' Caregivers abdicate the caregiving role, experiencing themselves as out of control and in turn become hostile/helpless to protect the child. The child is being neglected and abused. This attachment pattern often develops within children who grow up with physical or mental abuse or have parents with difficult experiences from childhood and who therefore cannot interpret the child's signals correctly. They may get angry or scared when the baby cries, and the child experiences the parent as scary. Still, the child needs to connect to the parent, which leads to particularly severe relationship disorders even in adulthood. The need for professional help to break the pattern is most alarming in this group [41].

The importance of a secure attachment is well-known through worldwide research. The first thing I must do as a parent is to provide my child with everything that I can afford emotionally. I need to respond to my child's needs, be available and predictable, and show interest in my child. The child needs to feel its value both physically and mentally from the beginning of life. The experiences that the child acquires very early in life, he or she will "remember" without the opportunity to later be able to explain or understand them. These are memories that lie on an unconscious level. Though, the body remembers.

An insecure connection may lead to behavioural problems later in life, for example, insecurity in close relationships, without the child – later the adult – having any idea of why. Nor does this person know how to deal with the

---

[41]https://www.psykologiguiden.se/rad-och-fakta/relationer/anknytning

problems for they cannot understand. The body only knows that 'closeness hurts' and that it is important to be aware in order to protect yourself. These experiences have their origins in a time before the child learns the language, which is why they cannot explain it. They had no language to create memories and understanding with [42].

Parents and relatives who are unable to connect emotionally with their children and therefore unable to provide them with a secure attachment should be documented and followed closely. That's my opinion. This is because you should be able to pay attention to children in time in families where such uncaring upbringing occurs. In case we do stumble upon such a home, we should put in people as support for rescuing children already at the beginning of life. Children who have not been given a secure attachment are also likely to have difficulties attaching to their own future children, which must be paid attention to before the vicious cycle continues.

---

[42] Pervin, L & Cervone, D (2010) *Personality. Theori and research.* New York: John Wiley and sons.

To keep an eye on this matter would perhaps be considered as a provocation by the Dandelion Children who become parents, but they would probably understand the explanation behind this very well. They themselves have experienced their childhood and have the confidence of knowing and showing that they grew up to be different from their parents.

If this had been done for the Norwegian mass murderer Anders Behring Breivik, many young people would probably be alive today who were murdered in cold blood on Utøya 2011. (Neither should we forget about his homemade bomb in Oslo, which killed eight innocent people the very same day.) From the testimony, we understand that he not only shot these people to kill, but he shot to injure first, then kill. When he was a child, he was one of these young people's future fellow human beings, we must not forget. A future fellow human being who did not get the help he needed. A future fellow human being whose personality became disordered and damaged to the worst possible extent.

Today's news has reported:

"The terrorist Anders Behring Breivik had personality disorders already as a two-year-old, according to documents that Norwegian TV 2 has taken part of. The mass murders on Utøya and in Oslo were likely to be avoided if Breivik had received the appropriate treatment, says the psychologist who investigated Breivik as a child. The documents also show that he, as a child, was rejected by his mother, who is said to have projected her sexual fantasies on him and called him both evil and wicked. Norway's foremost expert in child psychology wanted Breivik to be forcibly taken away from his mother in the years 1983 and 1984. The psychologist at the State Centre for child and youth psychiatry, SSBU, who in the 80's, observed the interaction between mother and her child, was heard by the police after the 2011 terrorist attacks: *"It is a tragedy that nothing was done about the care situation at the time because Anders's development, in that case, would have been completely different. At its peak, this is an extreme expression of the price society is forced to pay for having such a weak Child Welfare (Social Services), "* the psychologist said during the interrogations." [43]

I assume the people who are most likely to discover insecure attachment and dysfunctional parenting are

---

[43]https://omni.se/psykologen-breivik-hade-storning-som-tvaaring/a/K5ze

relatives of the family, as well as Child Welfare Centre. By spreading education regarding the understanding of behaviour, we can help more people see and understand these patterns, so they can be nipped in the bud. The first year in a child's life is a year that many people might believe isn't very important because of the fact that *"infants don't remember anyway."* As we have learned, research clearly shows the opposite. Traumatic experiences or deficiencies in the emotional connection between parents and child at this time may lead to the fact that the child in the future not will be able to feel empathy. A child who has to repress anger to keep parents satisfied and also because no adult is there to help him or her with their emotions and provide comfort is most likely to be devastated. The worst trauma a child can experience is not have one's basic needs met. It's like being sentenced to a life sentence where the child gets stuck in a psychic and physical imbalance for life [44].

The attachment theory, along with SOC and a favourable social heritage as mentioned, are extremely important factors that impact children's development the most.

---

[44]Rusz, E (2017 Relationspsykopater. Bladh by Bladh.

The Conscious Generation

I want to end this chapter with a few words of hope. A very conscious generation of children has now grown up. An increasing number of adult people agree with the fact that *you are not a parent just because you've had children. You also need to take care of them.* Previous generations may not have analysed their parents' parenting so closely, but now there is actually one grown child after another who emerges and expresses their experiences, feelings and insight regarding their upbringing. I assume that they then will become more stable parents themselves. This brings great hope. *Parents are no longer something that you just become, it's something you deserve to be.* I'm hoping for a revolution against and within the adult world, the adult world that doesn't take on responsibility. The fact that now-adult children more and more often go out with information about their childhood is something which we should see as a signal pointed directly at us who now have children growing up. Many of us just simply have to shape up, admit, and do something about our own problems, if we are having any, and take an impression from how other parents succeed in raising healthy children.

Though it can't be ignored that there are, in fact, many parents who really, really have serious problems, serious difficulties, *but* it is, in these situations, you as a parent to take on responsibility by asking others for help if you cannot seem to be enough for raising your child. In cases where parents do not realise themselves that they are destroying their children, society must step in.

Encouragement and Upbringing

Something that I want to say to every parent is: *Let your children get to choose their own path in life.* Encourage them to go their own way, and then support them as they set off. Help them grow their own chosen way. As I told you, dad wanted an education. Just like me, he wanted to study. My dear grandmother told me that. But he never got to it. Maybe at that time, in his family, it was not possible for financial reasons? That I don't know. He might just have been expected to be like his father. What would have happened if he had gone to the university? Got out of his home and had the chance to experience that other world that I eventually got to experience, got other impressions and life experiences, another kind of knowledge, a further perspective… I am convinced that one of the most important protective factors for me has been to succeed in school and get the chance to further my studies.

Instead, he took, maybe without questioning, and in accordance with his social heritage, the same profession as his father. That's when he lost his opportunity to see matters in a wider perspective since he by himself didn't seek anything outside his own sphere. Everything he saw and heard, he related to himself, not to others and their world, their experience or will. What was in his inner world was equal with facts for him, it doesn't matter if the facts were incomplete or out of context.

Sometimes children choose the same career path and interests as their parents. Of course, this is exactly the correct decision to make if the child really finds his or her great professional interest and hobbies in the same area as the parents. Some parents really inspire their children, you know. The opportunities for genuine growth are really in place then. BUT if the children feel an expectation from a parent to be on the same level as their parent, not only considering behavioural patterns but also professional career and interests in order for them to be sufficient, there is also a risk that jargon and of course personality passes on, even unhealthy ones.

I have been the only one sticking out in my family. I have experienced that I didn't belong, I had no place. Just like in that boat, when we approached the lock, I had no place. When I studied to be a teacher, I felt that I became one of those "strange people" who wasn't like my dad. The feeling of belonging, therefore, didn't exist for me.

A person with a personality disorder manages to present himself as incredibly strong. Incredibly, incredibly strong.

And correct and proper. I have repeatedly been amazed by their ability to be contagious, not only regarding children but also adults. They appear strong, so there is an unspoken "requirement" that you should be the same and have the same opinions to be good enough. They can sound demanding to other people, a very discouraging jargon, diminishing jargon towards the majority of people around them. You have to fit them; otherwise, they will not like you, and in a strange kind of way, most people are fooled to believe that it is important to be liked by that person. Most people want to be liked, of course, and therefore they fall into the trap and start striving for their approval. Fawn for them. I, with my insights, have been forced to stand as a witness, seeing one after the other disappearing. When I have tried to speak, nobody has listened.

I know that dad could influence people to be like him. Even adults. Somehow he made them believe what he said or thought was correct and important. He made them look up to him, and they may have felt unspoken demands to fit in. Now, I am talking about adults. Consider a child in this situation, then. With environmental impact over time, it's no mystery that it passes on from one generation to the next.

In the beginning, when it is a new contact, I have noticed that people line up to avoid falling into the category of diminishing, but over time one can surely notice that they begin to sound like, move like, and copy the same facial expressions and sarcasm as the narcissistic person next to them. Narcissistic people are so strong in their appearance that their children start to resemble them. School supports the *society values – be kind to each other, everybody has the rights to be heard, everyone's of equal value etc.* – but a parent who aggressively emphasises his personality and his opinions on a child is sometimes creating a perfect version of himself for the future.

Children should not become their parents even if they are healthy. They should become themselves. If they receive support in that direction, the chance increases for them to grow up as well-functional and happy people, who also in time are able to raise well-functional and happy children. They are given a chance to receive high levels of Sense of Coherence.

We can ask ourselves how children who are forced into one situation after another possibly could get the chance to reach a feeling of coherence in their lives. If nothing comes from within themselves, then, of course, we have a catch 22 when it comes to SOC. At least if they do not hold the resilience that Dandelion Children seem to have. Whether a child or a young person is your child, your nephew, your neighbour, your brother or sister, your student, it doesn't matter, continue to encourage and support them! If you notice that something is wrong, tell them. Provide them with the information that if they often feel bad, something is wrong. Tell them that we are free to feel what we want, think what we want as long as we don't hurt others. Every child should know that.

It does not always have to be the home situation that is dysfunctional. There may be other problems in children's lives, such as bullying, which surely has a negative – mental and emotional – effect on them.

For each and every person who finds their way in life and therefore also happiness, the world becomes a little better. I am living with a conviction that dad would have lived today if he had done as I did – left and gone his very own way as a young man and also received help with the areas I've written about above. Maybe he had also been a dear and present father to me and a dear and present grandfather to my children.

Some children of narcissistic parents choose to stay in their parent's presence far into adulthood. For me, it never would have been an advantage to stay. I had developed into a person who did not fit into dad's perception of how people should be, so I chose to go.

Raising Children Requires Knowledge

There are children of narcissistic parents who turn their crushed self-image against their selves. I did. I haven't ever done anything to hurt another person. Instead, I tormented myself as a consequence of my lacking self-esteem.

It is also known that narcissistic parents can also raise narcissistic children, as the children take a strong impression of the parent. They learn early in life that it is important to stay ahead, take matters into their own hands to compensate for their lack of self-esteem, and possibly thus become narcissistic themselves. It is likely that the most upset parents on the grandstand, those who emphasise their children most of all, defend their children most of all, but also inside the walls of the home bark at their children most of all if the match was lost, are narcissistic. They are ashamed of their children if things do not go well, and shame is the worst possible feeling they may experience.

If you find yourself a witness to this, try to talk to the child or the other parent. Co-dependency may make it impossible to reach them, but you still have a larger chance to reach through to them than trying to change a possibly narcissistic parent. If you choose to talk to a narcissistic parent first, you will never get close to the child or the partner ever again.

To avoid narcissism, we shouldn't either *be too* kind to our children, kind in such a way that we *spoil* them. Today it is said that the rates regarding narcissism are increasing. Many young people think that education, working, and providing for themselves can wait. They instead are being provided by their parents to be able to do everything they want, travel, and having fun. These children may grow up as people who hold their own perspective higher than everything else around them.

Even if research are telling us that narcissism is a disorder which derives from great damage in childhood and that it lies much deeper within a person than *"only thinking about yourself and only use your own perspective to lead your life,"* the behaviour is a warning signal. If we are to raise a generation with narcissistic behaviour or at least narcissistic tendencies, there is a strong cause for concern, for they are the ones to raise the next generation. We often raise our children to the top of the world and believe that we do them a favour when we as parents strengthen them so immensely that they both in our eyes and their own eyes simply are *the best!* Below I have collected five points that tell us what *not* to do as a parent. In fact, it is said that these points may also trigger narcissism within a child:

- To make them believe that they are infallible.
- To constantly compare them with others to show them that they are superior.
- To be a role model who cannot accept criticism.
- To brag over them and apologise for their shortcomings.
- Speak badly about children who are different or "inferior" [45].

Nor can it be ruled out that social media may include a risk regarding us raising a generation with narcissistic traits. If it is important to you to be seen and if it matters to you very highly to be interpreted as an important person, we ourselves can imagine that the constant pursuit of attention

---

[45]https://utforskasinnet.se/5-tecken-pa-att-du-uppfostrar-narcissistiska-barn/

on social media can reinforce the narcissistic traits in humans.

With these two contrasts in mind, I believe that we never can certainly know which path children of narcissistic parents will take. What have they taken an impression of? To disappear or becoming narcissistic themselves. We may be able to see quite early in life how they are affected. We should be paying attention to this matter. Of course, we should not raise our children the way dad raised us, not being noticed. Children should not live for their parents, children should be allowed to exist for their own sake. But we should also not make our children believe that they are, *yes indeed they are*, the only winners at the top of the world. Neither of these two approaches are okay, instead, we should raise our children to the best of our knowledge in this matter.

I get scared at the thought of raising my children to unreasonable heights and make them believe that they are the ones to always be at the forefront. Just think of the problems they will be having in romantic relationships in the future if I do. It is in a relationship quite crucial over time that one is able of both giving and receiving, be sensitive, humble, and understanding. This is important also in friendship and at work.

Likewise, I get scared at the thought of them telling me in adulthood that they were not seen by me when they were children. Being a parent is a balancing act, but it is important that we hold knowledge, self-esteem and self-confidence so that we can cope keeping this balance. All parents probably need to review themselves once in a while and sometimes also ask for advice.

I was at a lecture with Kent Hedevåg when he told his listeners how wrong it might turn out when we take for granted that young people can cope when they reach puberty. *They have become "almost adults" now. They are going to high school!* We will be wrong in this matter because of the fact that their brains are under "reorganisation," their entire lives are under construction. For parents to be present, helping them through this remodel is, of course, of great meaning. To me, this is not the same as "spoiling" them. We understand that we have to separate one thing from another.

Further, since many people are talking about today's parents creating a narcissistic generation, I guess too many of us have taught our children that they are very, very special and that they have rights, rights, and rights. They have the right to demand, and demand, and demand. If you don't receive what you want, something is wrong, and you are a victim. Of course, then it is somebody's fault, and you ought to be compensated, compensated and compensated. Everyone should be successful, beautiful and achieve financial success. Some of them want to put in as little effort as possible to reach their goals but glow and shine in a blinding manner when they are seen or heard. We are teaching our children that rights are more important than obligations, and everything ought to be fun and easy in life.

When these young people later in life become parents, it continues but may turn the other way around. Then the dysfunctional context will turn up again, which we have seen earlier in this book. Parents who are having narcissistic traits or are used to only be thinking of themselves and having fun in life can hardly cope with the effort that comes with nurturing and supporting a child through the early, critical phases of life. They can hardly cope in giving them a secure attachment and handle the little ones' defiance periods.

To what extent a parent manages to support the child considering shame, is said to be the most crucial factor regarding child developing narcissism or not. A narcissistic parent infects the child with shame because he or she is unable to bear shame and guilt within oneself. As an environmental heritage, the risk is obvious regarding the children growing up with exactly the same shortcomings as the parents. *Nothing will ever be their fault again either.*

It will never be okay to yell at a child, make it feel ashamed, and later not be mature enough to reconcile in the name of love. Narcissism is a growing and very worrying problem. No wonder our society can be experienced as colder than earlier if narcissistic influences flourish all over. Talking about shame, I came up with the following idea:

We shall teach our children to separate right from wrong without putting them in a state of burning shame so that they will be able to feel ashamed as adults without becoming defensive if they do something wrong. By saying this, I don't mean that it is a good thing to feel ashamed as an adult either, but it is still noticeable in a manner of bad conscience. People who are able to experience and accept a bad conscience may, to a wider extent, apologise and change their behaviour if they have gone too far in a situation. That is a phenomenon with great importance. Great, great importance.

I have found some questions for you to consider as a parent:

- Can your child respect you, not just because you are a parent, but also for your way of living?
- Do you show respect for your child's individuality?
- Do you know when your child really needs you, and are you there for him or her on those occasions?
- Do you keep track of what your child is up to?
- Do you stimulate your child to think for oneself?
- Are you giving your child the opportunity to build one's character, traits?
- Are you making it clear to your child what values you stand up for and what expectations you are having on your teenager?
- Are you giving your child increased privileges and more freedom when you see signs of greater maturity?
- Can you admit to your child that you are wrong sometimes? [46]

Think about it. Review yourself. It is important to dare to do that once in a while.

---

[46]Hotchkiss, S (2008) *Why is it always about you?* The Free Press.

Wisdom

Wisdom is a concept that we sometimes use without reflection. It is a concept that fits well with the message within this book. Wisdom mainly involves three points:

- You need to have knowledge.
- You need to have the ability to make decisions.
- You need to have the ability to make decisions that are good for others.

(Psychiatrist Simon Kyaga)

We talk a lot about IQ (Intelligence Quotient), but a less known concept that I often believe is much more essential is EQ (Emotional Quotient), which my dad lacked.

People with empathy, compassion for others have, according to both research and reason itself, much greater chances of succeeding in life than those who lack EQ. For example: Who would like to have a full-blooded egoist at one's workplace who doesn't see or show any compassion for others? No matter how high levels of IQ this person has, I don't appreciate having him or her close to me anyway. Nor in a private context or in a close relationship.

It happens that people confuse wisdom with high levels of IQ. That is wrong. I cannot imagine a wise person who

285

has high levels of IQ but lack EQ – a wise person who is insensitive or evil. To be able to act within the best interests of others is a part of what we teach children in school. It is a message meant to reach all the students during their time in education. *To be able to act in the best interests of others.* Work with this as a parent too. When our children meet, they then will meet kindness in life, and find hope for a good future. Remember that being able to act in the best interest of others, doesn't necessarily mean that you need to forget about yourself and your own wellbeing.

Do You Smell a Rat Regarding Yourself?

Have you discovered anything about yourself so far? Do you recognise yourself somewhere in this book? Think about it. I myself could have become narcissistic. Would it, in that case, have been *my fault*? It is not possible to write a book like this one without giving you a heavy dose of truths about your damaging behaviour towards others. However, the question is, is it your fault from the very beginning? No, not originally. However, we cannot have a society where it is okay to not take on responsibility for our own actions.

To the Narcissistic Person

The corner of shame

There is an imminent risk that if individuals with narcissistic traits recognise themselves - they will not appreciate what I'm writing. They may experience that I'm putting them into the corner of shame, a place which for them is worse than hell itself.

However, that is not my ultimate purpose. I wish that as many of these individuals as possible can see that this corner is a dead end and that they can come out of it and enter the light where most of the rest of us are.

Could dad have been helped? Could his suicide have been avoided if he had realised that the corner of shame, which he fought so hard to avoid, not even had to exist in his life? In our lives…

And when was it too late?

Eva

In case you are a narcissistic person or have the tendency to become one, here are some tips for you. First of all, learn to take on responsibility for your actions yourself. Do not put the blame for everything that goes wrong on someone else's shoulders. You and your behaviour is something that you yourself have to work with. However, you can always seek help, such as in the form of counselling. You must let old miseries out, but then it is up to you to take on responsibility and change your behaviour for the better.

I have heard an adult narcissistic person can discover things about himself. I, therefore, know that it is possible for you to discover the problems within yourself. This person was terrified after reading about growing up in a narcissistic family, and he started wondering if he too had become one who:

- Boasts and exaggerates his talents and successes (grandiose)

- Believes to be special or superior to others and requires to be treated with great respect

- Requires a lot of attention, praise and admiration from others

- Puts his/her own needs first and takes advantage of others

- Has difficulties putting him or herself into other people's situation (no empathy, does not care)

- Is at first perceived as a charismatic and exciting person in his/her social life, but then turns into arrogant and condescending when he/she receives a setback.

(Jenny Klefbom, psychologist)

…and he decided to seek help from a psychologist. This is probably the critical point for the person. What would he do now? Will he strengthen his narcissistic defences, or is there enough will and wisdom in him to go through treatment? After all, the treatment is demanding and will go deep down into his soul. He may feel very bad for a period of time, but maybe he has to walk through the fire to free himself from his thoughts, which could be:

- Why don't people get it?!
- Why is the world full of worthless idiots?!
- Why don't they do as I please?!
- I'll give a shit about her!!!
- I have to talk about this amazing thing I accomplished so that everyone can hear and see it!!
- Why don't they see it?!
- How can they not care about my efforts?! They are ungrateful!!
- I know I was the best!! Why didn't I win? Are they against me?!! I'll show them!!
- I'm gonna have that piece of the cake!!

If it sounds like this inside your head, it will make you do things that will have people distance themselves from you eventually. This can definitely lead to people not liking you for a long time, especially once they discover how you are. You get bitter and tell yourself that they are just a bunch of idiots. Over time, the bitterness will be all over you, and people will flee even faster. When that happens, the confirmation which you are consciously or unconsciously looking for in your surroundings seems to you increasingly distant (I here refer to the end of the book). There is a risk that this will not end well at all.

Narcissistic individuals are everywhere described as human beings who just think in terms of I, me and mine. Yes, that is how I know you too, but I have understood, after dad's tragic death, that you are living in a constant struggle that hurts you too. With ageing, it will probably get even worse if you don't stop it. You often perceive that you are treated unfairly. People see you in a way that you don't wish to be seen. This seems to be the whole narcissistic dilemma: You are dependent on others to see you in a certain way because you don't have a truly positive view of yourself. This is something, though, that you won't admit in the first place. Perhaps you don't even know about it.

That reminds me of my dad. The older he got, the more often he switched homes. He moved because he wasn't satisfied with the people living in the same village or town. You know, *there were nicer people in the next village or town*. When he moved there and lived there for a while, they too turned out to be ungrateful idiots, and he moved again. If he didn't get the response he wanted, he got tired of everything in his life. I don't think that he ever considered that the problem could lie with him and not everybody around him.

When we talk about narcissism, what happens is that the person, in this particular case you, who possibly was badly treated as a child by their narcissistic or intoxicated parents, get stuck in a *see me and feel sorry for me-behaviour* for the rest of your life. There are no chances for a person to feel good in such psychological imprisonment. However, there is a completely different world to discover beyond the darkness that has followed you since childhood. Some of you might have been experiencing abuse since you got home from the maternity hospital. You have bad memories saved in your minds. You don't always even remember what happened to you because you had no words to create memories with.

If you are one of those children who had experienced abuse, it will probably create problems for you, and you will need support to be able to understand yourself better and make the necessary changes. In case you remember some bad memories from childhood years, the risk is that an "inner critic" has got a hold of you. You hear voices from the past, which are tormenting you, telling you that you are worthless. You do everything you can to prove that you are better than that. So far, it is quite all right. However, when you go even further, and you do everything to prove that you are *better and more important than everyone and belittle other people along the way*, that's when it goes wrong; rather, too wrong for anyone wanting to be by your side. The risk is overwhelming for them staying with you just because you have taken power over them.

Once people around you have realised how you are, they may leave you alone very soon. In time, you may start believing that the voices of the inner critic are, in fact, other people talking, people who are present in your life right now. Narcissistic people sometimes develop schizophrenia as they age.

If you open up about yourself, there is always someone who can listen. It could be a friend if you haven't lost everyone at this stage or a psychologist with whose assistance you may be able to win your friends back in due time or find new ones to really bond with in a genuine kind of relationship – a wonderful thing that you may not yet have experienced so far. If you think there aren't many people who can really understand you, you are probably right. It's true that not many people are able to understand your suffering. I hope you can put your finger on it and work with it. You have something to share that people also need to know. Your voice is one of the most important of all in this very matter. You can help to make the world a better place by getting out of your prison.

Another thing for you to consider is that you believe you are better at a number of things than your friends, but there are also things that you are worse at. The thing is, it doesn't matter at all. It is not those things that determine who you are and what value you have. At least not if you want to feel good and find real value in life. This is not the right way to look at things, especially if you want to find people who want to be with you, just because you are you.

I think if my dad had started reading this book, he would not have come so far as you. He had snorted and thought, *"This is bullshit!"* Perhaps he had even thrown the book into the fireplace. Dad liked fires, cosy fires in the fireplace, that is. Anyway, the risk of a narcissistic person reading this and thinking, *"This is still not about me,"* is overwhelming. Am I giving my dad an undeserved interpretation now? Am I thinking less of him right now? I will never know.

To the Psychopathic Person

I have an important message for the psychopathic people reading this book. First, learn to take responsibility for your behaviour. Do not put it on someone else's shoulders. You and your behaviour is something that you yourself have to work with. However, you can always seek help.

There are people around you who claim that you are suffering. If you really are, the rest of us don't know. Only you know, but it doesn't help you to manipulate the psychologist. Some psychopathic individuals actually know that they are psychopathic and are being dragged to a psychologist or a therapist by someone who still loves them. I don't know if you enjoy hurting others, if you feel good about it as some people believe, or if you are mean to them just because you believe that is the only way to get what you want. Your modus operandi is threatening, lying and even abusing. These are your ways to get what you want. However, these won't help you in the long run.

When it comes to meeting people in an acceptable way, you will not get anywhere without realising that you are different from many others. Only when you do that will you be able to retain people around you. Let's know yourself better with the help of this behaviour list about you:

- Considerable superficial charm
- Absence of delusions
- Absence of anxiety

- Unreliability, disregard for obligations, no sense of responsibility
- Untruthfulness and insincerity
- Antisocial behaviour
- Inadequately motivated antisocial behaviour
- Poor judgement and failure to learn from experience
- Pathological egocentricity. Total self-centeredness and an incapacity for real love and attachment
- General poverty of deep and lasting emotions
- Lack of any true insight; inability to see oneself as others do
- Ingratitude for any special considerations, kindness and trust
- Fantastic and objectionable behaviour
- No history of genuine suicide attempts
- An impersonal, trivial and poorly integrated sex life
- Failure to have a life plan and to live in any ordered way (unless it is for destructive purposes or a sham.

(Hervey Cleckley, Psychiatrist and pioneer in the field of psychopathy)

This is the information about you that is available in almost all the resources of psychopathy. After having learnt so much about people with psychopathic traits, I realise that it is probably futile to write this part of the book. The reason is that psychopathic people do not want to emphasise or understand anything that doesn't directly benefit them, and what I am writing now is probably not interesting in that manner. As I wrote earlier in this book, a person with psychopathy has stated, *"I do not feel that way, but I know you normal people do."* She thus improved her life, understanding that she was not like "everyone else," and adapted to make things work.

As a child, she learned the difference between right and wrong and she probably had a good childhood. Can you learn the difference between right and wrong as an adult? Can you, as an adult psychopathic person, repair yourself or learn to handle memories from a miserable childhood? The forces from inside, which may lead to aggressive outbursts, derive from a terrible childhood, according to several researchers. Researchers have suggested that people with abnormalities in the brain, something even you may have, can learn to function by knowing the difference between right and wrong. Some also believe that empathy and compassion can be acquired, so stay hopeful. With empathy, it will be possible to have a bad conscience, and with this comes morality.

When people meet a person who behaves like a psychopathic individual, they usually get the advice: *"Run! Do not try to save a psychopath, do not try to get a psychopath to understand you because it's not possible! Just get going!"* This is my experience too, so I join the ranks: *Run!*

The thing is that you also get to run from one place to another because you risk that they will no longer want your presence in the workplace, for instance. Sooner or later, you will be revealed. Literature about you says that you just keep on going and repeating yourself in other workplaces where you also risk dismissal. If you are a manager, then you might have to adjust to an unreasonably high staff turnover in your company.

The repercussions of your behaviour can occur in any form. For example, you may get fired by the partner you've tormented lately, but you might just run to find a new one or continue to torment your ex-partner. You manipulate others to make them stay with you. You lie and deprive others of their happiness and so on, and you may become provoked if you are reading this against all odds. No one will want to stay with you or feel good about staying with you, if you don't, as an adult, start studying the difference between right and wrong and modify your behaviour accordingly. You may also sit down with a psychologist and talk honestly about your life. What is right and what is wrong maybe something that you can't identify, but you can learn to find them out. The adults around you in your childhood should have taught you this from the start. Or, it may be that you know this very well, but instead of using this knowledge in a genuine kind of way, you pretend to seem infallible as long as you believe you need to get what you want.

You may not want to change; it's your choice, after all. However, if you don't even try, set your mind to the fact that no one will want to stay in your life for long if you decide to cover your ears up now. Your children would not want to see you when they have grown up, probably not your grandchildren either. The nasty part is that I don't know if you even care. It is said that you just want your children so that you can use them in a way that benefits you, and you call this love. It could be that you are trying to attract a new, child-loving partner by taking care of your cute children or that you receive money for taking care of them, the same money you later spend on your own. If emotions are foreign to you, you have to learn what is okay and what is not.

If you are having these abnormalities in the brain that researchers have discovered or if you have grown up with parents who created these traits within you, then there is the explanation. It cannot be said to be "your fault" from the very beginning. However, everyone must be made responsible for their own actions, and that includes you too.

There are therapists and psychologists who believe they can help you gain a well-functioning life. I hope you have somebody in your life who hasn't yet given up hope on you, and they may help you get some kind of professional help, and you listen to them without trying to manipulate them. After treatment, you cannot pretend that you have changed in order to continue your psychopathic behaviour. You will be revealed again and again. You probably have heard this: *What goes around, comes around.*

The Hope

If we don't act when children are very young and if we have the attitude that we *can not determine anything about a child's personality – we have to wait for them to grow up before we know...* Raise your hands, everyone who believes that these people will seek help by themselves as eighteen-year-olds… As you have read, individuals with personality disorders don't even consider the fact that something could be wrong with them. Within five or ten years, the children/young people we have let down will raise the next generation of antisocial children. Basically, I am still a rather optimistic person, who usually refuses to give up, so I still think I might have succeeded in reaching through to one or two of them after writing my last chapter. Hope is the last thing to abandon us, and that is important!

In this book, you have now received a lot of negative information, which is too dense. I hope, though, that you have seen hope in between the lines. A part of the hope for the future now lies within you, in the knowledge you have acquired. It is only when we have the knowledge and become aware that we can start acting for a better future. Without knowledge, we are lost. How should we be able to solve a gigantic problem if most people don't seem to see it or understand it?

Many problems where children are victims can be alleviated with money. We have a lot of charity going on, and we can help with our donations. In this book, though, we have a problem that can't be remedied with money. This requires completely different efforts from us fellow human beings. Maybe you have your own thoughts about what you think is needed to be done in this issue. It is a positive thing if you reveal a situation in your vicinity and have thoughts about how you can help right here and now.

Those who have knowledge of our global environmental problems say that we have many solutions to the problems already. Likewise, I say that we have many solutions to save our children also from abuse, but there are some things that need to change.

Attention

Maybe you think your chances of bumping into a person with a personality disorder are low. However, whenever we open up and talk about this issue in a group, there is someone or the other who has been in contact with such an individual. They have met a person who made them feel bad, uncomfortable, inadequate, exploited, manipulated or even scared. What's more common is that they have a friend who has been victimised by a completely incomprehensible human being. However, they often don't understand what is happening and why it is happening. Then truth is that things you don't know much about don't hit you right away, and you avoid taking strict actions. Consequently, you engage in constant lamentation and mental anxiety.

To avoid those negative responses, help each other to spread information. This way, we all can have a chance to help our fellows or receive their help to save ourselves in case we are being victims of someone's narcissistic tendencies. By helping each other and be aware of people's behaviour, we will learn to see and interpret signals, namely to pay attention.

The Power to Influence

I am a person who works very closely with people who are suffering, and that gives me meaning. I'm proud of it because I know that I have helped people in my vicinity to get out of very serious problems. I know that this book has helped people even before it was published. Such is the reach of attention. We must not lose faith in our power to affect and influence. Our presence in the real life of the people is what will lead to a change for the better.

Stop the Family Secrets

The silence within the family, the oppression, the shame attached with getting help become enormous barriers in the way of reaching out to the right people. As we know, a person with one of these personality disorders can disguise their "personality" so that people outside the family can in no way believe that a completely different person lives within the walls of the home. I myself have been deceived over and over again in that regard. If I hadn't studied and experienced this illness so deeply and known the ins and outs of it, I would have been deceived to this day.

My grandfather was a charming and very nice man, but that was him only outside the home. Inside, he caused a lot of damage, *and* in this case, some people in the village knew about it. Dad could also be charming outside our home or even inside when he had friends over. I can still laugh at some of his jokes as his humour was amazing at times. He even cooked for parties probably because he wanted to gather praise from others. My mum often got to hear what an amazing husband she had. In our everyday life, though, he wouldn't cook or care about doing the dishes.

I have often heard about family situations worse than ours. One of the times, I was informed that the wife was sleeping in a caravan in the garden but had the nicest husband in the world… Yes, the stark contradiction raises questions. It should raise questions. The hope for the future lies with people who don't only make answers in their heads and stop inquiring. In this regard, you should be careful not to talk to your acquaintances about it in an irresponsible way only because that could become something we call gossip and lose meaning. Gossip may, of course, make things worse for the victims. If something seems strange, you should instead find out more about it in order to make a positive change. However, you don't have to do this alone. Reach out for help from somebody who really cares about such situations.

Do not risk your own life, but still, never think that you should avoid interfering in other people's lives when you smell a rat. I also got to hear that when I contacted social services in my teens to seek help for a friend who had called me to say goodbye. She was going to end her life. I knew how wrong things were in her life. I knew why she wanted to do it. But adults told me to not interfere in her personal life. I did it anyway to save a life. If I had not, how would I be able to sleep peacefully at night?

We may think that it is convenient to shut our eyes, close the door and just be happy. I'm not saying that that attitude is easy to change as it seems deeply ingrained in our bodies and our souls. However, with every single person who manages to change, the hope for a brighter future goes up. I used to hear the saying *"Nobody will ever remember a coward"* and laughed about it a little, but to be honest, I deeply feel that the day I die, I want to be remembered as a person who has fought for the good and for the right.

Stop the Lack of Knowledge

We can not expect ourselves and others to be able to help out when we barely know anything about the problem at hand. I'm talking about the lack of knowledge regarding personality disorders. Narcissism and psychopathy are topics that have been extensively discussed in books and papers, but there is still so much ignorance surrounding them. How often have you heard the following: *"A psychopath? Yes, that is a serial killer, isn't it?"* Or even worse: When we come across a driver making a dangerous passing, we hear people exclaiming, *"Fucking psychopath!!!"* Most psychopathic individuals do not fall into any of these categories of people. They are in our midst, and we often identify them too late. Their agenda is to extract whatever they can from other people in their lives before their truth comes out. They may have demolished an entire workplace, or they may have an adult child who has been subjected to abuse in childhood.

Everyone who works with children in different capacities should collect more knowledge about these families and children. We don't want families to get stuck in such a situation and suffer till the end. We don't want a new version of Anders Behring Breivik to come. We wish our children to have a good present and future as fellow human beings. When many people know that there is something wrong with a parent, such as the parent has served imprisonment for child abuse, and the other healthy parent begs for help to put a stop to the abuse, you know what is wrong. With the help of the powerful tool that knowledge is, you can bring hope into the equation by doing something meaningful for the family.

Stop the Paralysis of Action on the Boat, 'Society'

It seems we have a kind of paralysis of action on our entire boat, 'Society', in which we all are sitting. To be able to curb this menace in a successful manner, we should invest in our children. If we see recurring negative behaviour patterns within a child, such as antisocial behaviour, lack of guilt and shame, emotional coldness, lying or other deceptive behaviours, or fearlessness, we should take action to help them. If we see a child with bruises that seem to have been caused by the use of force, we should act. If the wife is sleeping in the caravan in the garden, we need to start wondering what made her do that. If someone comes and tell you about the uncanny behaviour of a person they have met, we need to believe in him or her and inquire more about it.

As I told you earlier, it would have been difficult to discover my family and rescue us when we were suffering from the same. However, we do meet children and adolescents with stomach pain, stress and headaches at times. We also come across young people who seem 'stiff' and are afraid of making mistakes. Throughout my high-school years and also through college, I have lived with headaches caused by tension, gastric catarrh and stress day and night. I ate lots of pills, and I spent almost all my time studying along with performance anxiety and my worried friends by my side.

When we meet such children and young people, we should ask how they feel. What does their self-image look like? They need to know their rights to experience life the way they deserve. Do they have a sense of coherence? Are they aware of the fact that there may be a background to why they are having those many problems? When I was seventeen, I got a neck massage from a physiotherapist. She said that I had been so stressed for so long that it had contracted into nodules that needed to be massaged to disappear. I later realised that she knew what was wrong with me. She started talking about my dad with me. Later, it turned out that she was the daughter of a man who knew my dad too well. I remember dad not being happy about me meeting with her, nor was he happy about me talking to a therapist. He was afraid, of course, because he suspected I talked about him. So, I guess deep down inside, he knew or understood that he wasn't a supporting and loving father. Sadly, he never thought about seeking help.

These problems run deep in our society. None of us can solve the problems that arise in the wake of personality disorders on our own. No civilian, no politician, not even the king of the world, no matter how powerful he is, can solve these problems by himself. We must keep in mind that there are many of us who are able to act and that we can help one child after the other and move on to the adults gradually to help them out in the same manner.

Imagine each adult helping one child each. What a change we could create! Imagine a world without these problems. That is the world we want to pass on to our children and grandchildren! A world with a lower risk of being cheated, abused, raped or murdered is a world most of us take for granted, but to accomplish that, we need to be curing multiple things. If some adults consider raising their ambition a little and help more than one child, well then we would reach our target in no time. If all the heroes come to rescue the world, we will probably relieve social services, the police, the health care, the prisons etc., in unimaginable ways.

We can reach our target by increasing the reporting of cases involving a personality disordered individual dramatically. That we can do when the reporter is given the right to conceal their identity. That is, they do not have to reveal their identity while reporting a case. It would be very helpful to have people come in groups and report their suspicions. We can do it together. Then in continuation, we also should be allowed to testify in groups, if it comes to that. These situations are so frightening sometimes that no one should be left without support. Imagine multiple people reporting strange things that seem to happen in a house down the street. It feels better than approaching the case separately, doesn't it? Those who set the rules could consider this. What is most important? That the hidden statistics are revealed or that people have to sit alone against potentially threatening and dangerous people in the courtroom testimony?

When a case arrives at court, and it is time to review the evidence, lawyers and judges need knowledge of personality disorders to deliver justice. The strange behaviour of the potential disordered person can not be taken out of context. That these cases end with *"All people lie once in a while,"* *"All people exploit others once in a while,"* *"All people lack empathy once in a while,"* is hardly okay. Also, the outcome should not depend on who is judging. Those involved should put the pieces of the puzzle together and exploit their knowledge to see through the situation and also consider how this destructiveness will affect the children and the partner. Then, we will see our judicial system changing for the better and cast positive implications for the world over. We must not forget that in the change lies hope for a better future.

The Heritage

Considering the fact that personality disorders may be inherited from one generation to another, and there is a lack of power of action, the number of affected people around us would only increase. Remember that we can put a stop to it with the help of knowledge, attention, commitment, courage and action.

Often, the destructive patterns within families constitute the negative social legacies we often see. Right now, we are living with so many narcissistic people around us that we cannot imagine their number. We are talking about "a generation of spoiled children and young people," young people without self-examination and perspective. They are also a generation that is growing up in an alternative world called social media to an unreasonable extent. Their survival is about being seen. This is probably a breeding ground for narcissism, even if the worst kind of narcissism is said to derive from abuse in childhood. None of us has probably missed the suspicion that social media may be responsible for the many mental illnesses that are there in children and young people. The hollowness that some of these young people seem to suffer from reminds me of the hollowness caused by narcissism. You don't feel satisfied with yourself and your life. Therefore, you have to be seen by others all the time if it's possible. Ideally, you also wish to be the best and the most popular. Otherwise, you will not feel calm and happy with yourself.

The hope lies in the fact that we, as parents, understand the significance of the upbringing we provide our children. We need to inform parents that they should not put their children on top of the world as being the best in everything. This is because either they will be hit hard when they meet the actual grown-up world, a world where they suddenly have to take on responsibility, or they will develop narcissistic traits and attitude as their last resort to seek reassurance about their image from the world. If you, as a parent, know that you have pampered your children unreasonably, and you're now having problems with setting limits for your child, and you can't fix the situation by yourself, you must seek help in due time. You can approach the family centre, for example. Things are still in your hands to a large extent, even if your child has reached the teens.

Another area for parents to pay attention to is SOC – The Sense of Coherence. Reflect for a while and think of what *you* can do to help your child with this incredibly important area of their lives. Sometimes, only a few sentences are required to redirect your child's thoughts to where they should be and ignite new ideas that help them. The power of a parent's full attention and warmth is invincible. Parents caring and also setting proper limits is a perfect concept. Conversing with the child about matters and problems and trying to put yourself in the child's shoes is also a great part of the receipt, along with the healthy limits. Parents usually continue to reflect on their children's behaviours and responses once they get aware of them. In such people, we have great hopes that our future will be brighter.

The Law

Sometimes we end up at a certain point where parents lose their rights to take care of their children. Sometimes, however, they have no child to take care of when this point falls in. By then, the child no longer lives with them because he/she has succumbed to death. Parent's rights to their child sometimes seem to overweigh the rights and the safety of the child. As I said, sometimes, it continues until the child's last day in this world.

We have many kind-hearted people who have chosen their profession to help others. Children's fate sometimes depends on us, but when we suffer from paralysis, the important information never reaches through. Fortunately, there are some kind-hearted people who aren't satisfied with the law and question its purpose. That poses a serious question for our lawmakers. It's a problem that we, you and I, can't carry around on our shoulders. All the statesmen should also read a book about personality disorders in order to familiarise themselves with the problems that often arise in these cases. It is necessary that the law supports *children* instead of supporting dysfunctional parent's rights on their children. It is necessary to have reasonable laws for a better future.

Researchers' Work

Researchers have, as I've mentioned many times before, established that there are abnormalities in the brain of psychopathic individuals. Perhaps more surprising is their claim that people with exactly the same abnormalities are in the midst of us and function well. Researchers are also doing research on human morality. They are looking for answers to the question, *"When does a child learn the difference between right and wrong?"*

That is where one of the points I have in my heart comes in: *Is it possible to stop or at least modify personality disorders for the better while children still are young?* Research has shown that it is possible. Think about the

315

difference it would make if all parents, school staff and everyone working with the youngest of our children learn more about these disorders and if they could use this knowledge to influence the children's empathic abilities. Today, these children may often be treated with hatred and experience distancing at the hands of both children and adults because their problem isn't understood. If they are met with a lack of empathy and routine anger from adults and other children, it will become impossible for them to create empathy and understanding within themselves.

In the best of worlds, all these children would be identified in time, taught the difference between right and wrong, taught the social codes and conduct, even if they don't *feel* to be acting in a particular way. It would go a long way in fixing their thoughts and actions.

In the best version of our world, we would detect psychopathic parents and protect children from them. People who have found out that they have differences in the brain but still function in our society together with other people, of course, have grown up in safe homes and received early warmth, love and knowledge of social codes.

In the best version of our world, we could stop narcissism by exposing the dysfunctional parents, and work intensively to give the children a new social heritage to be influenced by, a secure attachment, a Sense of Coherence, self-esteem, social codes and a fair idea of how the world should work. We could provide them with access to a security-giving, supporting person as a role model instead of the dysfunctional parent.

Now, do not forget what you've learned about the social heritage and the Sense of Coherence. This book is not only about *protecting children from* destructive adults but also about helping them in refraining from becoming one. Researchers have given us knowledge which we now need to put into practice.

The Adults

There are people who quite strongly emphasise that psychopathy cannot be treated. I understand that they are referring to the people who have already grown up and suffer from this disorder. But when we emphasise the hopelessness regarding the treatment of psychopathy so vehemently and at the same time ignore the researchers who say otherwise, then that's not right. It scares me that the general perception highly disfavours the children who can still be detected and helped, and these would be deprived of the attention they need if the belief regarding the impossibility of treatment persists.

The concept of "psychopathy" has also been misused to such an extent that no one dares to talk about it. The diagnosis does not feel reasonable in any case, so *"to be sure, let's just exclude it, rule it out."* Again, there are those who believe that psychopathy isn't a diagnosis but deviant antisocial behaviour. Regardless of that, people need to know what can be done about it. Stephen Wong, who is a specialist in the treatment of people with psychopathy, believes that it is not possible to change adult psychopathic individuals so much, but it is possible to reduce their propensity for violence and antisocial behaviour. They will always be psychopathic, but we can make them "nicer ones." Karolina Sörman, a researcher in psychopathy at the Karolinska Institute in Sweden, says that empathy exists within psychopathic individuals, but they choose to turn it off when it suits them. Likewise, they are able to turn the empathic ability on if they see a benefit in it. It should, in that case, be possible to train and increase their empathic abilities. Hope exists as it seems, and as a relative, it's nice to know that. But it will never work if we allow them to continue their rampaging and, by that, show them that their way to lead their lives is passable.

If a psychopathic person comes for treatment, the therapist should be cautious and not be fooled by their manipulation and exciting stories. He should also be strong and trustworthy for the patient. We also understand that the psychopathic person himself must be willing to receive help. All of these things together can produce positive results.

When it comes to narcissism, I will never know if dad could have been helped if I or someone else had got him talking about his problem. I don't think that as a young boy, dad showed any clear signs of developing narcissistic traits. I've been told that he was a very kind and well-behaved boy. He probably had no other choice than to be well-behaved. However, I know that more than fifty years after dad's birth, there were people in the village he grew up in who still remembered how badly grandfather treated his family. Decades after decades have passed. People talked. No one acted. Now we know better, right?

I know that narcissistic individuals sometimes seek therapy to make their lives work better. It is a shame that dad didn't realise that. Most people do not. The only consolation I have is that there is some hope for the future now that we have more awareness regarding mental ailments. When we talk about narcissism, we sometimes see that therapists miss the diagnosis because it doesn't fit into the short-term structure of care. Narcissistic people sometimes seek help regarding depression, anxiety, problems in relationships, or work-related stress, but they do not know they have a personality disorder [41]. When therapists miss this, they also miss the chance to help a person who has been abused since childhood, who may really be wondering what is wrong with him, and who may have children of his/her own.

Here, we also find some glimpses of hope if any therapist, counsellor, psychiatrist, or psychologist reads this. I must share a short story with you:

"A person actually, and unbelievably, discovers that he might be narcissistic. Hope lights up when he says that he is going to see a psychologist. His relatives think that now it will probably get better. Six months later, all hell breaks loose, though. Narcissism had increased to unimaginable measures, and no one could spend time with this person any longer. It appears that the psychologist for six months has

---

[41] Hotchkiss, S (2008) *Why is it always about you?* The Free Press.

confirmed that this narcissist was a victim. A victim since childhood. A victim of external circumstances. Now, this man has buried himself deeper in that belief.

What the relatives see as a result of the treatment is an extremely reinforced narcissistic defence, which destroys all hope that their relative would ever recover. "

The treatment this man received is called Psychodynamic Therapy. It aims to explore how events in the past have affected the individual and require the person to recall his past in grave detail. It often confirms the patient's misery because of the things that happened in childhood which is, of course, relieving since old misery must be let out. It may be trauma speaking in these cases. The significance of Psychodynamic Therapy can't be disregard. In fact, it has helped me and many others a lot to talk about and analyse the past.

However, people with narcissism and psychopathy, not at least those with Histrionic Personality Disorder, which is said to be a female variety of psychopathy, are masters in exaggerating and lying. If the therapist does not see through this, there is probably a risk of reinforcing the patient's feelings of being a victim since childhood, which happens when they talk about events that didn't even happen in the first place. According to the relatives, what happened was that the man in the above story lost sight of reality. He began to hate everything and everyone because he was *a victim*, now a full-time victim. His memories became blurred, and there was then room for the dramatic behaviour that personality disordered individuals sometimes carry around. Maybe he could no longer distinguish dream from reality, and of course, there was also a diagnosis that pointed toward the same thing.

When I think of Aaron Antonovsky and SOC, Sense of Coherence, I can see a direct connection with Cognitive Behavioural Therapy. It aims at getting the clients to look ahead in life, avoid seeing themselves as victims and instead figure out how to act so as to improve their lives in the future.

Is Psychodynamic Therapy or Cognitive Behavioural Therapy the best for a narcissistic person? Maybe a combination of these two is needed? The past is there within us, and we need to talk about it, but can it be risky to exclude Cognitive Behavioural Therapy, the part where you really are looking ahead? *What do I do about my situation? Horrible things have happened to me that explain, and we can talk about it, but how can I myself also influence my future? How can it get better? How can I handle it?*

These are common questions in Cognitive Behavioural Therapy. When I sought help from a counsellor, she happened to be a Cognitive Behavioural therapist. Today, I am very happy about it. You know the story about juice and lemons by now.

Well, maybe it is a completely different treatment that is needed in really serious cases? How many experts on this are available in our country? These are some of the many questions that pop up in our heads sometimes. I hope that someone in the previous mentioned professional groups holds the answers to them and start working more intensely in reaching out to the rest of us with the information.

The number one way to succeed in this regard is, of course, to see through narcissism and psychopathy. As I said, however, there is evidence that that is not always the case in health care. It is not diagnosed in the short-term structure of care. How can we then succeed?

In this chapter, I am collecting hope for the future. I am focusing on which factors can or at least need to change. We need to be aware of where we best turn for help, both as a personality disordered person and a victim.

To You Who Discovered That You Have Been Affected – Old and Young

If you're suffering at the hands of a psychopathic person, I sincerely hope your mind is a bit clearer after reading this book or other literature about psychopathy. You know what you have to do:

You have to find a way to break the pattern and the relationship. Furthermore, you have to find ways to grow as a human being again. You have to think about the lives and future of your potential children. It's a very heavy responsibility. Bring a book, this one or another, under your arm and find someone who'd give you the greatest confidence to tell your story. If you aren't lucky to find someone who understands or listen, then leave the book on their desk and return in a week.

If you live with a narcissistic person, I hope that you realise in time, and not when forty years of your life have passed with you living for another human being and not for your own self. You need to find a way to grow as a human being and also need to think about how it has turned out for your children. You need to use knowledge about children and the development of young people to help them to lead a healthy mental life – help them to become Dandelion Children, at least.

I have dedicated my life to the children. Today's children and the future children. As a psychology student and as a teacher, I am interested in learning how destructive patterns where children are involved could be broken. It is a matter of immense pride to me if my job as a teacher or my passion for writing can help at least one person to break the social heritage, a destructive relationship, an unreasonable custody dispute, or their own narcissism… Yes, it is a big deal. An entire family in the future may be affected by one single person passing on the inheritance. This person may toxify everyone's life around him. I am one of many witnesses of the impact it can have on others.

The close relatives, parents, siblings, and adult children of people with a personality disorder must not be forgotten in this book. They are also among the victims. If I meet a partner, who doesn't seem stable enough, I can choose to leave him or her hopefully. However, it's not that simple with blood-band relatives. If I have an adult child with a personality disorder, of course, I wouldn't want to nail my door for him or her. I hope that something I have written can help you too. I understand that you want to do everything to save your son or daughter, brother or sister or your parent from a dysfunctional life. Do not wait in that case. I know from personal experience that narcissism has a tendency to deepen over the years. However, maintain your distance and never ruin your life by trying to help another human being who does not want your help.

When it dawned on me that I had been affected while growing up, I really went down for a long period of time. I was mentally unbalanced. I attempted self-starvation, had headaches around the clock, stressed in an unreasonable manner… until one morning when I couldn't get out of bed. I was nineteen years old and did not yet know that I grew up in a narcissistic home. The problems were still going on back home, and childhood memories bubbled up as flashbacks. I had clear memories of my childhood trauma, so much so that it almost felt like old happenings became alive and started playing before my eyes many years later. The sounds in these memories were as clear as they were when they took place. I lived in my memories. As a person, I was devastated.

Self Help

I think literature about how to help oneself sometimes receive unjust criticism. I have acquired many wise thoughts from such books, which have supported me on my way to strengthen my self-esteem, and this has been absolutely crucial in my life. If you have big problems in life, every little piece of advice you can get can alleviate your ailments and get you closer to living a peaceful life.

Therefore, I would strongly advise you to look for literature that can help you. There are so many wise people around the world who have written their thoughts down. I realised the importance of self-help when I was over thirty, and I began to explore answers to my problems, which were mainly stress-related at that time. I had to do something about my problems for the sake of my children. That is when I really broke my social heritage. Through these wise authors and with support from my husband and friends, I could help myself out of the darkness and achieve self-esteem. Today, I do not evaluate myself on the basis of my achievements or appearance. I work because I find it fun, interesting and valuable for me and those around me. Today, I am completely unpretentious and calm within myself. I don't need any praise or confirmation from others. Of course, it feels good if someone applauds me for things I do well. I am not indifferent to people's opinions, but they don't affect me that much in the negative sense. I constantly remind myself that it is dangerous to put your value on some performance indicators, and it is also dangerous to put your value in the hands of others.

I mourn the fact that my dad never got to experience the same feeling of peace and quiet in his soul that I now have got the chance to experience. He missed the good in life and never got to experience the life he wanted. He did not understand it back then and never sought any help. He did not read self-help literature; neither did he go to a therapist. Perhaps he was not as lucky as I am. In his youth, there was little, if any, awareness among ordinary people on the topics of narcissism and psychopathy. The same was the case with my grandfather. My grandmother wondered what was wrong with him. They may have concluded it was 'Bad childhood,' which is far from enough an explanation for his queer behaviour. Both dad and grandfather would have needed help as children.

Find Your Life

You can never flee from your past. It will catch up with you if you try. You have to face your sorrows and memories. Question, cry, scream and think, because when you have faced it, it is time to move on. Explore new ways of thinking. You will learn to see yourself in a different light. You will learn new methods of dealing with life situations.

When you find the way of thinking that helps you become a healthier or a better person for yourself in any way, try to activate them over and over again until your brain has reorganised and learned to go there automatically. I hold my sandwich just as I wish nowadays, remember? When you reprogram your brain, you will receive a clear sign when that you wake up one morning, and you fail to understand how on earth you always have been thinking, or you simply can't remember how you have been thinking earlier.

Probably, in the aches of yourself, you will find a great life experience. Decide what to do with it.

A way of thinking, which has helped me a lot is, *"Okay, where does life want to take me by putting this on my shoulders? Where does life want to take me by putting me into this situation? What is life's intention by making me meet this horrible person? Is it because life wants me to take out a new direction? Change my career? Help people in the very same situation? Write a book? Start lecturing? Do something new, which really inspires ME? Do something for my children?"* It is a way of thinking that may help you make juice out of the lemons life throws at you and enjoy it. It surely has helped me. This is the way you can focus on opportunities instead of getting depressed about the situation

329

at hand. Of course, you *are* a victim. Allow yourself to sometimes be what you, in fact, are, *a victim*, but don't get stuck there. Hopefully, you will get tired of that way of thinking because it really is boring in the long run.

I'm not a religious woman, but once, a dear friend of mine told me, *"Keep your head up. God gives his hardest battles to his strongest soldiers."* I don't know where she had heard it, but that is also a statement that has helped me sail through the winds a lot of times.

Now, it is probably not enough to get away from a destructive environment. As I wrote earlier, we have to work with our shattered self-image. 'WHO you really are' becomes an important question. That self-reflection is the crucial factor that dad and grandfather missed as young people, so it became too late for them to get back on track, but I picked it up. Here's some advice along the way:

- Learn the difference between forgiveness and understanding. Nobody will ever force you to forgive, but *understanding* the situation, on the other hand, will help you through hard times.
- Take on no blame for things you haven't done. Try to see clearly. You will go from 'worthless' (as you've been taught you are) to valuable.

- Create your own image of how you want your life to be.

- You may have lost your faith regarding the existence of the good World. Collect all the goodness that you see in other people. Bad memories will be exchanged for new and better ones.

- Keep your distance from those who are trying to steer you so that you get the psychological space you need to grow.

- Find healthy people – good friends and a good partner to share life with.

- A very good piece of advice I have received is to practise your breathing with support from medical yoga. There are many exercises that provide a calmness to the body that may help you in difficult situations.

- Think of the personality disordered people as two-year-olds regarding emotional level, but don't feel sorry for them. No crawling back, remember. It is the person with the personality disorder who should take responsibility for their own actions, after all. You may want to be 'the bigger person,' but a disordered person will eventually get to you, no matter how great you are, you will be torn apart.

- Work immensely with your self-esteem. Read books about this important topic. It may be absolutely crucial for the rest of your life.

- Set plans in action, and make sure you are having fun once and a while!

Finally – The Ageing Narcissist

Before dad's death, I saw what became of him in the end. He limped, and he was in pain. Parkinson's disease inherited from his grandfather also affected him. He had become, or had in fact always been, impossible to work with, so he had no job. He had burned the rest of us out in the family one by one - first, me and later my siblings and my mom. There was a time where we all kissed his feet. That time had passed. I quote two passages that I read and found very striking:

"The narcissist perceives ageing almost as an insult. It is partial dissatisfaction with his own body defects that arouse his discomfort. The sick or ageing body arouses disgust. It simply doesn't fit into his worldview. He may not say it, but when others think, *"When I die,"* the narcissist thinks, *"If I die."* To die would be the absolute greatest violation of all."

"When the mirror reflection speaks its clear language, a crisis can be triggered within the narcissist. Especially if he is sick, his wife dies, or he loses his job. That's when he may need to apply for help in psychotherapy or psychoanalysis. But when he no longer can close his eyes to the passage of time and the people around him no longer show respect or appreciation, it is most likely that he strengthens his narcissistic defence. Now he appears in all his rawness, envy, egocentricity and downgrading of others. It is often difficult to understand that his increasing egoism is an attempt to recreate the time when he was in the centre and was superior to all others and that he now is trying to force this feeling to return. It is even more difficult to understand that the growing narcissistic behaviour is also an attempt to maintain a psychological balance. He is set on defending his self-respect to the last drop of blood. Otherwise, there is only emptiness left. When he is no longer able to maintain the image of himself as superior to all others, he literally falls apart. Shame washes over him and sweeps all defences. That is the faith of the ageing narcissist." [42]

My dad probably reached this stage on the beautiful summer day in July 2018. The narcissistic poisoning that was caused

---

[42] Sigrell, B & Teurnell, L (2011) *Narcissism – jag, mig och mitt*. Lind & Co.

within him as a young boy finally led to his death. *Dad was one of those children who didn't manage to save themselves.*

A Significant Insight

Dad. I was angry with you for a long time. You never saw me. Nothing that happened in my life was big enough for you to notice. That's how I experienced it. I longed for your attention, your pride in me being your daughter. I fought all the way into adulthood to feel that I was important to you. What I did not know back then was that my real problem was that I wanted your help building self-esteem, but everything was always on your terms. I was forced to realise that it never would happen. You would never help me have an individual identity.

The question is, how could you help me build something which you never got the chance to build yourself? Just as I can't teach my children or give them something I don't possess, so couldn't you. I realised that gradually when I wrote this book. I am sorry that you had to leave this world with your hands full of the sourest lemons.

I promise to continue to take good care of your grandchildren. I try to help them create such a life as you probably deep down wanted but didn't know how to create - a life that you probably wish for in *your next chapter*.

Despite a lot of suffering, I am deeply moved by your story.

Your daughter Eva.

References

Antonovsky, A (2005) *Hälsans mysterium*. Natur och kultur Akademisk.

Cleckley, H (1988) *The mask of Sanity*. Echo point Books & Media.

Engström, L & F (2012) *Vad får maskrosorna att växa?* Umeå universitet.

Heilskov, Bo (2014) *Beteendeproblem i skolan*. Natur och kultur.

Hotchkiss, S (2008) *Why is it Always About You? The Seven Deadly Sins of Narcissism*. The Free Press.

Kreis, M, Hoff. H.A, Belfrage, H & Hart, S (2016) *Psykopati*. Studentlitteratur.

Näslund G.K (2004) *Lär känna psykopaten*. Natur och kultur.

Pervin, L & Cervone, D (2010) *Personality. Theory And Research*. New York: John Wiley and sons.

Rusz, E (2017 Relationspsykopater. Bladh by Bladh.

Sigrell, B & Teurnell, L (2011) *Narcissism – jag, mig och mitt*. Lind & Co.

https://aktivt-valmående.se/?p=61

https://dodadekvinnor.story.aftonbladet.se

https://www.forskning.se/2017/09/14/insatser-kan-motverka-psykisk-ohalsa-vid-aggressivt-antisocialt-beteende/

https://giftigarelationer.com/2018/03/18/delad-vardnad-med-en-narcissist-det-ar-sallan-samma-barn-som-du-lamnade-som-kommer-hem/

https://giftigarelationer.com/2017/11/29/skillnad-pa-narcissist-och-psykopat-vad-finns-dar-bakom/

https://lattattlara.com/klinisk-psykologi/KASAM/

https://omni.se/psykologen-breivik-hade-storning-som-tvaaring/a/K5ze

https://www.psykologiguiden.se/rad-och-fakta/relationer/anknytning_/
https://sites.uea.ac.uk/providingasecurebase/attachment-patterns

https://www.psykologiguiden.se/rad-och-fakta/symtom-och-besvar/personlighetsstorningar/psykopati

https://utforskasinnet.se/5-tecken-pa-att-du-uppfostrar-narcissistiska-barn/

https://www.vardfokus.se/webbnyheter/2018/maj/foraldrar-vill-aterkalla-barns-adhd-diagnoser/

P3 Relationsradion, Karolina Sörman – Forskare Psykopati vid Karolinska institutet.